CW00925406

NL.

Business Decisions and Strategy

Theme 3 for Edexcel Business A level Year 2

BURNTWOOD SCHOOL
BURNTWOOD LANE
TOOTING, LONDON
SW17 0AQ
TEL : 020 8946-6201
info@burntwoodschool.com

**Polly Glegg, Alan Hewison,
Paul Rapley and Nancy Wall**

Edited by: **Nancy Wall**

Polly Glegg is a lecturer in business and economics education at UCL Institute of Education in London, where she is completing doctoral studies with a focus on business education. Before this she taught business studies and other subjects in London schools for 11 years, including as an Advanced Skills Teacher. Polly has contributed to textbooks and publicly shared teaching/learning materials for a number of years. She is also a regular contributor to resources produced by the Economics, Business and Enterprise Association.

Alan Hewison is an experienced teacher and has been a senior examiner of economics and business for many years. He has been involved with the development of some of the new economics and business courses and has written several other revision guides and textbooks.

Paul Rapley is an experienced teacher of Business Studies and Economics, having taught both subjects to A level for nearly 20 years in a number of schools. He has written articles on subjects ranging from motivation to international competitiveness and has been published in Business Review and Teaching Business and Economics. In addition he reviews books for the Economics, Business and Enterprise Association for whom he is also a trustee. He has worked for some of the major awarding bodies in different capacities and has a particular interest in coaching to improve teaching and learning.

Nancy Wall was a teacher for 15 years. Since 1991 she has worked in curriculum development, with a particular interest in teaching strategies and classroom resource development. She is currently reviews editor of 'Teaching Business and Economics', the magazine of the Economics, Business and Enterprise Association. She has long experience of writing and editing resources for students.

© Anforme Ltd 2016
ISBN 978-1-78014-032-2
Images supplied by Shutterstock.com

Anforme Ltd, Stocksfield Hall, Stocksfield, Northumberland NE43 7TN.

Typeset by George Wishart & Associates, Whitley Bay.
Printed by Potts Print (UK) Ltd.

Contents

Using this book

In studying the content of Theme 3 Business, you need to be able to draw on a great deal of what you learnt in Year 1 of the course. Sometimes you are reminded to **revise** certain ideas from Themes 1 and 2 that you really need to have grasped, in order to understand the new content. Other times, you are given a **cross reference** to remind you of something that you already studied in Theme 3. Do not ignore these tips! Many aspects of Business are linked to other topics; the more you can identify these links, the better. **Key terms** have highlighted definitions in this book, but not for ideas that you learnt about in Themes 1 and 2. You are expected to understand these already. Constant and regular revision will help!

You need to be *able* to apply all this knowledge in different and sometimes unfamiliar contexts. Specifically, for Theme 3, you must demonstrate your ability to use the knowledge you have gained to **calculate, analyse** and **evaluate** in the context of the pre-released case study.

There are many questions in this book; some of the numerical ones have answers (if there are answers, you will be given page numbers). The questions are mostly designed to help you to discuss and to learn. So there are very few questions with mark schemes.

You can use past examination papers and mark schemes to help you become familiar with the style of questions used and how marks are allocated. The mark schemes in particular will show what the examiner is looking for in each response. The Principal Examiner's reports give an insight into what is expected from candidates and therefore provide a very useful resource for improving examination technique.

> **Tip**
> You can download past examination materials, free of charge, from your examination board's website.

Analysis and evaluation are particularly important skills in Year 2. When you see the word **analyse**, start by describing and defining the relevant business terminology. The key to good marks here is to ensure that you develop your comments by, for example, explaining 'why' or 'how' they are relevant to the situation under discussion. Do not waste valuable time by attempting to evaluate this type of question. A well-developed analysis applied to the scenario is all that is required.

Longer response questions usually require a thorough **evaluation** of a specific business situation, or problem, associated with the case study, before arriving at a decision. As well as considering the causes, costs and/or consequences of the situation, you must consider the positive and negative aspects. It may be more logical to discuss both the positive and negative implications of a point as it arises. However, some candidates prefer to consider, for instance, several positive aspects before looking at the negative ones (or vice versa). Both ways are acceptable, however, the key to achieving high marks is to expand fully all the points you have raised before arriving at a conclusion. Simple lists of advantages and disadvantages will not allow access to the higher level marks.

> **Tip**
> Each question on your examination paper requires a particular style of response. You can improve your understanding of the response required by looking at three aspects of each question:
>
> ● The command word.
> ● The marks available for the question.
> ● The theory that you are asked to use in the question.
>
> Always support your conclusions with evidence. Consider the short term impact of a decision versus its long term impact. Weigh up the relative benefits of different outcomes.

The content of this book is potentially very interesting. Try hard to read around the subject, using other books, websites and media generally. Gather a range of points of view. Work hard and learn all you can from as many different sources as possible.

Chapter 1

Corporate objectives

Your objectives

You may or may not have thought about your future life yet. If you have, then you may have some rather vague long term ideas such as a long and healthy life, a successful career, to be rich or to be happy and preferably both! Alongside that will be some more medium term objectives which indicate how you might begin to realise these ambitions, such as getting to a university or securing a place on a training scheme. Before that, you may be thinking about your exams next year and the grades you need to achieve to get to a university. Right now, there are likely to be other targets such as end of term grades, doing well in a test and so on. Then there are even more immediate goals, such as finishing your homework.

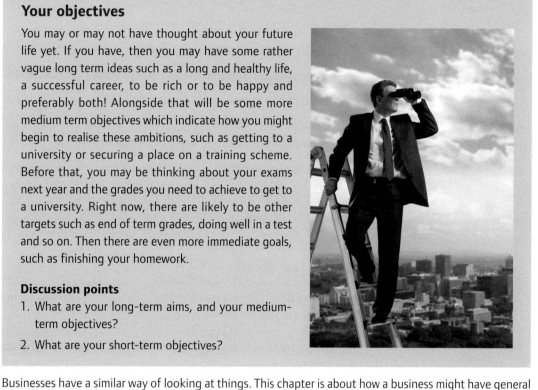

Discussion points

1. What are your long-term aims, and your medium-term objectives?

2. What are your short-term objectives?

Businesses have a similar way of looking at things. This chapter is about how a business might have general long term objectives which can be broken down into identifiable, measurable objectives and targets. It has a hierarchy running down from aims, to mission, objectives, strategies and tactics. The latter are the means by which the business will actually achieve its aims and objectives.

Aims

Business aims are very broad, long term ideas as to how the business should develop. They can sound rather vague and open to interpretation. They may be statements of intent such as to be the biggest or the best at something. They may reflect ethical values and ambitions and they will certainly change over time as the business grows and its direction changes.

GSK (Glaxo Smith Klein) is a UK pharmaceutical company and the sixth largest in the world. It aims to *"Increase growth, reduce risk and improve its long-term financial performance."* All very worthwhile aims but they tell you very little about just how GSK will achieve them. In fact those aims could apply to just about any other business.

Mission statements

Many businesses try to express their aims in a **mission statement**. In this way their aims can be made inspirational and motivating, suggesting a vision that highlights a common purpose.

● The mission statement reflects the main purpose and principle of the business.

● It states what the business is, what it does and its direction.

● Employees and other stakeholders should be able to understand the mission statement easily.

> **Business aims** are long-term intentions that describe the fundamental purpose of the organisation.
>
> A **mission statement** is a short sentence or paragraph to explain, in simple and concise terms, the aims of the business and the reasons why it exists.

Mission statements

Bearing in mind the description of a mission statement, look at the following examples:

1. Decide whether they satisfy the criteria of a mission statement.

2. Which do you think is the most effective and why?

3. Which do you think is the least effective and why?

One Team. One Plan. One Goal – *Ford*

To organize the world's information and make it universally accessible and useful – *Google*

To inspire and nurture the human spirit – one person, one cup and one neighbourhood at a time – *Starbucks*

To bring inspiration and innovation to every athlete in the world – *Nike*

To give people the power to share and make the world more open and connected – *Facebook*

Saving people money so they can live better – *Walmart*

To provide a profitable airline where people love to fly and people love to work – *Virgin*

Corporate objectives

Corporate objectives are derived from the aims and mission statement. They are more precise and set out goals and targets that the business wants to achieve. They should be practical, specific and measurable, so that the business can judge the success or otherwise of its efforts to achieve these objectives. As well as defining ambitious targets for the business as a whole, subsidiary objectives will apply to individual departments and business functions too.

> **Corporate objective** – a well-defined, realistic and measurable goal, set by a company, that often influences its internal strategic decisions.

GSK sets out four main corporate objectives…

Objective	Measure of success
To grow a diversified global business	• £23bn Group turnover • 40% Group turnover outside USA and Europe
To deliver more products of value	• 4 significant new product approvals in 2014 • Around 40 new molecular entities in phase II and III
To simplify the operating model	• 33 days increase in working capital • £3.5bn cumulative annual savings made through restructuring programmes since 2008
To be a responsible business	• 1st in 2014 Access to Medicines Index • 84% Dow Jones Sustainability Index score

Note that these objectives are ongoing. Just because GSK has achieved '40% Group turnover outside USA and Europe' does not mean it will stop trying to diversify. These corporate objectives lead on to more specific and detailed objectives. For example, as part of its corporate objective to diversify, GSK may have a specific target of increasing sales in SE Asia by 15% over the next five years. That in turn leads on to other objectives that are more precise still, such as growth targets for each country within SE Asia.

Corporate objectives should be **SMART** – this is an acronym for **S**pecific, **M**easurable, **A**chievable, **R**elevant and **T**ime-bound. There are several different forms of SMART but they all mean the same thing.

Targets

Diversifying

SMART

	Specific To simply say 'to improve quality' is not good enough. Being specific would mean saying 'to reduce the quantity of our products with defects'. This lets everyone know what needs to be done.
S	
M	**Measurable** This means being specific by saying that the intention is 'to reduce the quantity of our products with defects to 3%'.
A	**Achievable** The idea of reducing defects to 3% has to be realistic and within the capabilities of the business i.e. achievable and not some hopelessly optimistic wish.
R	**Relevant** This is about choosing objectives that matter. There is little point in reducing defects if the product itself is nearing the end of its life cycle. It may be much more worthwhile to develop a new one.
T	**Time-bound** This sets a time period in which to achieve the objective which helps to focus efforts and measure success e.g. 'to reduce the quantity of our products with defects to 3% within 6 months'.

Measuring success

The end result is an objective that is clear to everyone, within the capabilities of the business and there is a clear end target that success, or otherwise, can be measured against.

Critical appraisal of mission statements/corporate aims

Aspirations

Mission statements can be seen as written expressions of corporate aims describing the overall aspirations of the business. They set out what the business does and how they are going to meet the needs of the customer. They are intended for all stakeholders, although the customer is usually the main focus. They are written in qualitative terms, designed to show the business in a positive light. Mission statements are also intended to create a sense of unity and common purpose amongst employees and encourage them to work together for the good of the business and to achieve its corporate aims. They can also be statements of ethical principles and practices.

Ethical issues

Mission statements are sometimes criticised as little more than window dressing, fine words designed to make the company look good and improve their image. They take time and money to create so are they worth it?

Benefits of a mission statement

Productivity

● A simple and clear mission statement can act as a motivational tool within the business. It can encourage employees to work together towards one common goal that benefits both the organisation and themselves. A good mission statement helps to engender job satisfaction and motivation, leading to increased productivity.

● It signifies clear intent and direction and acts as a signal to all stakeholders that the business knows what it is doing and is on the right track. It is this sense of coherence and stability that is perhaps the mission statement's most important attribute.

Drawbacks of a mission statement

Sir Richard Branson once said that *"Most mission statements are full of blah truisms and are anything but inspirational."* For many businesses the mission statement may be too vague or unrealistic to be of use. How can the purpose of a business be condensed into a few lines or sentences?

● A business may want its mission statement to sound good but its main purpose is to get people to do things. An unrealistic mission statement can actually be de-motivating; employees may struggle to meet its demands and it may lead the business to make unwise decisions.

● Mission statements have also been criticised as a waste of time and money; those resources could be better used in other areas of the business. In short, a mission statement may be no more than a PR exercise.

Public relations

> ### Think!
>
> GSK's mission statement is *"Our mission is to help people do more, feel better, live longer."*
>
> In February 2016 GSK was fined £37.6m by the Competition & Markets Authority (CMA) for 'illegal behaviour' in relation to its antidepressant drug Seroxat, which resulted in higher costs for the NHS.
>
> The CMA said that GSK had paid generic drug producers more than £50m between 2001 and 2004 in return for their delaying the launch of cheaper versions of the drug. This meant that GSK could continue to charge higher prices to the NHS and other customers.
>
> Now go back and read that mission statement again!

Exam style questions

Caterpillar

Caterpillar is the world's leading manufacturer of construction and mining equipment, diesel and natural gas engines, industrial gas turbines and diesel-electric locomotives. Founded in California in 1925, the company has more than 110,000 employees. Caterpillar machinery is recognisable by its trademark 'Caterpillar Yellow' livery and the 'CAT' logo, which has now been licensed for a wide range of clothing and other consumer products.

Caterpillar's mission statement is a combination of four missions that inform strategies and decisions. In brief, the company's mission statement is *"To provide the best value to customers, grow a profitable business, develop and reward people, and encourage social responsibility."*

1. In your own words explain the difference between a mission statement and a corporate objective. *(4 marks)*

2. Explain the reason for Caterpillar having a mission statement. *(4 marks)*

SMART objectives

3. Suggest two SMART corporate objectives that Caterpillar could develop from its mission statement. *(8 marks)*

4. Assess the value of a mission statement to a business such as Caterpillar. *(10 marks)*

Chapter 2
Theories of corporate strategy

Terms to revise: the design mix, the Boston matrix, product differentiation, the product portfolio.

Aston Martin strategic developments in products and production

In 1913 Lionel Martin and Robert Bamford founded Aston Martin in Warwickshire. Lionel Martin was a race car driver and the idea was to make performance cars to beat their rivals. By staying relatively small and exclusive, the company was allowed to grow slowly, even surviving near bankruptcy in the period between the world wars. The Ford Motor Company became the majority shareholder in 1987 and even today Ford own 8% of Aston Martin shares. The company has stuck rigidly to its strategy of exclusivity and quality; since it was founded only approximately 70,000 cars have been made, and 90% of these are still in existence.

Location

In February 2016 the company announced that it would build its new DBX in a brand new facility in St. Athan in the Vale of Glamorgan in Wales. This is a major coup for Wales; it took two years to secure the deal ahead of 20 locations around the world. Construction of the factory will begin in 2017, and cars will begin rolling off the production line in 2020.

To survive at the luxury end of the market, the company has been looking at broadening its range to appeal to younger customers, especially women. The car, which is an all-electric 4x4 and is expected to cost £160,000, was unveiled at the Geneva Motor Show in 2015. Dr Andy Palmer, Chief Executive, said the company envisaged a world "…*when luxury GT travel is not only stylish and luxurious but also more practical, family friendly and environmentally responsible.*"

Collaboration

At the same time, the company has announced a partnership with LeEco, the Chinese backer of the electric car start-up company Faraday Future. The strategy is to develop a production version of the RapidE concept vehicle although they have said there is the 'potential' to make other cars in the future. To this end Faraday has announced plans to build a production facility in Las Vegas. Aston Martin, despite having a century of experience in developing performance cars, is behind the game compared to companies like Ford and Nissan when it comes to producing electric vehicles.

The Chinese government has said it wants five million electric vehicles on its roads by 2020, and is trying to offer incentives to drivers such as exemption from the law that says non-electric vehicles can only be driven on Beijing's roads six days a week. LeEco is currently known in China for its on-demand LeEcoTV service and Le smartphones. This joint venture intends to bring the RapidE to market by 2018.

Discussion points
1. To what extent do you think locating the production facility for the DBX in Wales is crucial for maintaining the Aston Martin brand?
2. Aston Martin is clearly thinking about long term growth. Explain how working in partnership can open up opportunities, helping the company to be more successful than it would be acting alone.

Developing a corporate strategy

Strategy and tactics

Johnson & Scholes, the strategy experts, state that "Strategy is the **direction** and **scope** of an organisation over the **long-term**: which achieves **advantage** for the organisation through its configuration of **resources** within a challenging **environment**, to meet the needs of **markets** and to fulfil **stakeholder** expectations." Although the distinction between aims and objectives has been blurred in recent years, it is still sensible to think of corporate strategy as a map which the firm should follow in order to achieve its objectives. Therefore firms will make strategic decisions which tend to be longer term and *tactical* decisions which tend to be shorter term, often reacting to changes in either the internal or external environment.

Product portfolios

Ansoff's Matrix

In 1957, Igor Ansoff presented his 'Strategies for Diversification' in the Harvard Business Review. His matrix has been seen as a useful model when looking at methods of growth.

Figure 2.1: Ansoff's Matrix

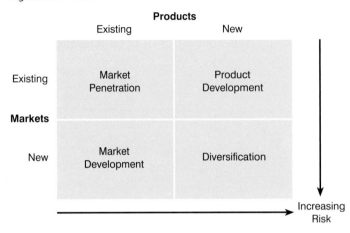

> **Ansoff's Matrix** helps businesses to analyse a range of possible options by considering their relative risks. The options relate to the product portfolio and possible new markets.

Marketing

Market penetration is the strategy of 'sticking to the knitting' and effectively means that a business continues to do what it has always done. This does not mean the business will not make any changes. It may be that it can continue with its core focus, but do it better, more cheaply, faster or more efficiently. (The Gucci story on page 10 is a good example of a market penetration strategy.) This is the least risky strategy according to Ansoff; current expertise is at its maximum, but only as long as the firm is robust enough to continue without making any significant changes to product or market. Aston Martin took this approach in its earlier years.

Market development is the strategy of finding new markets for existing products. Because knowledge of the new market may be limited it is considered more risky than market penetration. The market may be new in terms of both the geography (new country) and the demography (new customers in the existing country). In either case the best solution is often to seek strategic partnerships with experts in the new market. For example, the furniture giant Ikea has an online presence in just half of the 27 countries where it operates, but aims to expand this to the point where e-commerce could generate one fifth of sales by 2020.

Product development is the strategy of selling new products to existing customers. Whilst it carries the inherent risk associated with launching new products, any company adopting this strategy will have detailed knowledge of its customers and should, in theory at least, have worked with them on developing the product. Aston Martin's developments with performance electric cars could be seen as a product development strategy.

Diversification

Diversification, launching new products into new markets, is the strategy Ansoff describes as the riskiest. At the same time, this is the strategy which protects firms against over-exposure in existing markets. Remember that growth through diversification does not have to be *organic* (growing from within – more on this in Chapter 6). A firm could adopt a strategy of diversification by means of takeovers, as with Sainsbury's takeover of Argos.

When evaluating growth, according to Ansoff, it is always worth asking to what extent the strategy is part of a long term plan, or is it a tactical move, e.g. in response to changes in the environment? Is the firm leading or following the market? Is the strategy *balanced*? For example if you looked at Virgin Plc in terms of Ansoff's Matrix you could argue that by following relatively low risk strategies of market and product development, the business can afford to take the occasional journey into high risk, high profile ventures. If everything the company had done had been high risk would Virgin Plc be where it is now?

Think!
Like most of the theories in this chapter, Ansoff's matrix was developed at a time when the definitions of products and markets were very different to those of today. With e-commerce and globalisation fundamentally changing our understanding of what a market is, and with technological developments leading to more *virtual* products, do you think these models are still useful to decision makers?

Porter's Strategic Matrix

In his 1985 book 'Competitive Strategies', Michael Porter identified strategies in two areas:

● Looking at **competitive advantage** in terms of whether the product was high or low cost.

● Looking at **competitive scope** in terms of whether the target market was a broad or a niche market.

He called these 'generic strategies', because they can be applied to products or services in all industries, and to organisations of all sizes. These are ways of gaining competitive advantage – in other words, developing the 'edge' that gets one firm the sale and takes it away from the competitors.

Figure 2.2: Porter's Strategic Matrix

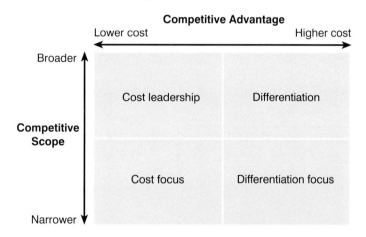

Cost leadership is not the same as price leadership. It could be a strategy of lowering costs in order to raise profit margins by not altering prices. Similarly it could be the strategy of seeking lower costs to allow it to reduce prices and therefore increase revenue (as with Aldi). For a firm to be able to adopt this strategy they must be confident they can gain an advantage that is difficult for the competition to copy. This could be brought about for example by investment in technology or outsourcing production.

Cost focus strategies involve niche markets and therefore the firm will need a thorough understanding of both the market and the changing conditions within it. In this case the business needs to understand the risks of focussing on a small section of the market.

Differentiation focus is again a risky strategy, requiring the business to offer something different within the niche where it operates. By concentrating on a niche market, the firm is able to develop a deep understanding of its customers and so secure a high degree of brand loyalty. If the strategy is carried out correctly it makes penetrating the market unattractive to competitors.

Differentiation involves making products or services more attractive and distinct from competing products. The exact way a business does this will depend on the nature of the industry and the product, but the key is to differentiate on a basis that customers value. This could include elements such as image, after-sales service, design or function. For this strategy to be successful firms will need close relationships with customers, good market research, effective R&D functions and a marketing strategy that successfully communicates the USP to the customer.

Gaining competitive advantage

Differentiation

Competitive pressure

Boston Matrix

> **Think!**
> To what extent can a firm pursue a differentiation strategy in the long term? What might the success of the strategy depend on?

Aims of portfolio analysis

There are very few companies that sell just one product. Most will have a range of products and over time they will bring out new ideas and stop making products that are no longer selling. Having a product portfolio means a firm will continually be making strategic decisions about which products need support, which are generating most revenue, and which need to be discontinued. For example footwear generates the most revenue for Adidas and Nike, despite both companies having a diverse product portfolio. Therefore the competitive pressure within the market means both firms need to continually revitalise their ranges by bringing in new product lines in place of old ones. In the example below Dell made the strategic decision that they are happy with their product portfolio as it is, and do not at this time want to make any significant changes.

> **Portfolio analysis** involves a business in considering each of its individual products, in the context of its market situation. The potential of each product will be assessed, in the light of its profitability, market position and distinctive features. Market research will help to explain both its performance and its potential.

The Boston Consulting Group created the Boston Matrix to help businesses organise their product portfolios in terms of whether the product market is actually growing (market growth) and the amount of that market controlled by the firm (market share).

Figure 2.3: The Boston Matrix

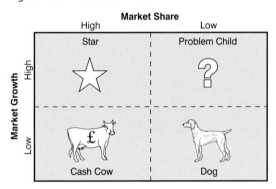

● **Star products** should stay dominant for as long as possible to develop brand identity. The appropriate strategy is to HOLD.

● **Problem child products** are often the stars of the future. With these products, the firm may have only a small foothold in a growing market. If products in this category are to turn into stars they often need a lot of attention and tend to be expensive in terms of resources. Firms will try to avoid problem child products turning directly into dogs. The appropriate strategy is to BUILD.

● **Cash cow products** are often at the maturity stage of the product life cycle. They often require less advertising but generate lots of revenue, which can then be used to support other areas. The appropriate strategy is to HARVEST.

● **Dog products** have a low market share in a market which is not growing. The business should seriously consider whether producing, marketing and retailing this product brings any benefit to the organisation. However it's not always that easy. Stopping production and diverting resources to other areas of the business takes time, money and careful planning, particularly if there is a human aspect and retraining or redundancy may be required. The appropriate strategy is to DIVEST.

> Putting it simply…. KILL THE DOGS, AND USE THE COWS, TO TURN THE CHILDREN, INTO STARS

Portfolio analysis

Dell predicts PC market consolidation and rules out smartphones

Michael Dell, CEO of Dell suggested Lenovo, Dell and HP will continue squeezing out smaller firms and will become increasingly dominant over the next 5 to 7 years. He also suggested that Dell is gaining market share compared to Lenovo and HP in the notebook market. Currently Lenovo holds top position with HP in second place in terms of global market share.

	3rd Quarter 2014	3rd Quarter 2015
Dell ('000 of units sold)	10,106	10,160
Total ('000 of units sold)	73,728	79,842

However the PC market has been declining for some time, with sales in the second quarter of 2015 being 9.5% lower than the previous year. Despite this, Dell believe they are in a position to grow further. The top three companies are following different strategies. HP is splitting into two companies, with one focusing on printing and hardware and the other on the enterprise market. Meanwhile Lenovo has acquired Motorola and is moving into the smartphone market, but Dell said *"I think there may be only one or two companies who make a profit in the smartphone business today, and there are quite a few that lose substantial sums of money. So no thank you. I do not want to be in the smartphone business."*

Source: Company accounts

Questions

(a) Calculate the percentage change in market size between the third quarter of 2014 and 2015.

(b) Calculate the percentage change in Dell's market share over the same period.

(c) Explain how Dell's product portfolio differs from those of Lenovo and HP and comment on the Dell strategy.

(d) Show how portfolio analysis might have been used by these companies to guide decision making.

Achieving competitive advantage through distinctive capabilities

John Kay, one of the UK's leading economists, explained that companies with distinctive capabilities have attributes which others don't have and cannot copy. There are three distinctive capabilities that a company can possess and use to achieve competitive advantage through relationships:

● **Architecture** refers to a structure of relational contacts within or around the organisation, involving customers, suppliers and employees.

● **Reputation** includes the customer experience, quality signals, guarantees, spreading by word of mouth, warranties, association with other brands and staking the reputation, once it is established.

● **Innovation** contributes, provided it leads to a stronger competitive advantage.

> **Distinctive capabilities** are the ideas and resources that contribute to competitive advantage. Taken together they provide a noticeable difference to the customer experience that competitors cannot easily copy.

Capability and challenge

Kay found that whilst most successful businesses were able to identify why they were successful, they were less able to explain the key steps that they had taken to achieve that success. He concluded that the overriding factor was the relationship between the capability of the organisation and the challenges the organisation faced and that therefore the foundations for success were unique to each individual company. It follows then, that if a company focuses on that uniqueness, it should be better equipped to deal with the challenges. To use one of Kay's examples, BMW has two distinctive capabilities, the branding and the engineering quality. By focussing relentlessly on these areas the company has maintained high profit margins and unbridled success. There was no magic formula or master plan, just a laser sharp focus on continuing to do what it did well and keeping abreast of new opportunities.

Creativity

Example

Gucci's sales jump 5% as new styles revive brand

The luxury fashion brand Gucci has seen a better than expected 5% rise in sales in the last three months of 2015. After two years of falling sales the Italian brand seems to have turned a corner. Kerning, the French owner of Gucci has attributed the improved performance to the appointment of new designer Alessandro Michele. In a statement the company said "the brand's new creative vision" had been well received and provided "fresh impetus". Kering's other brands also reported leaps in sales, with Yves Saint Laurent (YSL) up by over 27% and Puma by nearly 12%.

Choosing markets

However the extent to which a firm can transform distinctive capabilities into competitive advantages depends to some extent on the size of the market, suggesting that the wider an organisation is spread, the less able it will be to maintain its distinctive capabilities. The more competitive the market, the less opportunity for higher profit margins there are, so even a significant competitive advantage may not result in high profits. The key message to business when developing a strategy could be *"choose your markets carefully."*

Effect of strategic and tactical decisions on human, physical and financial resources

Strategic decisions reflect the long-term objectives of the whole company. They require considerable expertise and will usually result from a period of serious thinking about current and likely future circumstances. For example, a decision to invest in a major new product development would be strategic.

Tactical decisions are made to meet short-term objectives. They will contribute to the strategic plan of the organisation. They may also reflect a need to respond swiftly to unforeseen opportunities or threats, e.g. cutting prices in response to a competitor's actions.

Argos owner received rival takeover offer from South Africa

Home Retail Group, which owned Argos, found their company at the centre of a bidding war after the Sainsbury's offer of £1.3bn was overtaken by a £1.4bn bid from South African company Steinhoff. Argos owns the UK furniture chain Harvey's, making most of its products in developing countries and selling its furniture across Europe.

Sainsbury's on the other hand faces increasing competition in the supermarket industry, not least because of the market penetration by firms such as Aldi and Lidl. Taking over Argos would create the UK's largest food and non-food retailer of choice, according to Chief Executive Mike Coupe. He said the merger would generate savings of £120m, half of which would come from putting Argos stores into Sainsbury's supermarkets. In the event, the Sainsbury bid for Argos won; the take over went through.

Discussion point

What strategic and tactical decisions would confront Sainsbury's as it worked out how to merge the two companies?

Whether the business is making strategic or tactical decisions the managers will need to consider the impact of change on the **financial**, **human** and **physical** resources the business has. It may well be that in planning the implementation of a strategy, changes to the **resource mix** need to be considered, but this in itself may not be enough to guarantee success. As well as looking at the resources prior to implementing a strategy, the firm may well need to think about the potential effects the strategy will have on the operational areas *after* it has been implemented.

Financial management

Financial Resources concern the ability of the business to finance its chosen strategy. For example, some strategies will require investment in new products, distribution channels and production capacity, as well as extra working capital. This may place great strain on business finances, so the implementation needs very careful financial management. Using tools such as ratio analysis (Chapter 18) and investment appraisal (Chapter 10), a business can examine both the impact of its strategy on its finances and the potential benefits the strategy brings. By weighing up risk versus reward (including the risks of not pursuing a particular strategy) the firm can compare the relative impacts of different strategies.

Human Resources

With a new strategy, the essential questions might include:

● Will the business have the right number of employees in the right place with the right skills and at the right time?

Flexibility

● Is there a training cost? How would this compare with finding new recruits who already have the skills required?

● What impact would potential redundancies have on morale and labour turnover (Chapter 19)? Does the strategy need an accompanying workforce plan?

> **Example**
> Looking at Sainsbury's successful acquisition of Argos, how would their growth strategy affect the workforce of each organisation? The strategy involves opening Argos branches within Sainsburys stores. Would the staff be trained to work in either department, depending on demand? Will wage rates between the two be equal? Would there be redundancies?

Physical Resources refer to the operational factors concerned with premises, equipment and all the other practical requirements needed to meet customer needs effectively. Necessary physical resources for a given strategy might include:

● Production or retail facilities: capacity, flexibility, maintenance and delivery equipment.

● Marketing facilities: use of e-commerce platforms, distribution channels, promotion.

● Communication and information facilities: IT systems for operations and sales, internal and external means of communication.

Chapter 3

SWOT analysis

Supply chain

Competition

Primark, a clothing retailer with over 290 stores and 57,000 employees

Primark launched its first outlet in the USA in September 2015 in Boston. Seven other sites were planned for the north east of the country. A venture as big as this requires considerable strategic planning and before that can begin, the business strategists would have reviewed all aspects of the company's existing policies. It's fairly easy to imagine how Primark might have set out to do this. Identifying its strengths, weaknesses, opportunities and threats might lead to a set of lists.

Primark's first USA outlet in Boston.

Strengths

- Wide range of clothing
- Fashionable and 'on trend'
- Cheap and affordable
- Well-known brand name

Weaknesses

- Long and complex supply chain
- Almost exclusively based in EU
- Certain products appear poor in quality
- Poor customer service, long queues

Opportunities

- Emerging markets in Asia and South America
- Possible expansion into the USA
- Growing market for sportswear/leisurewear
- Develop and improve digital presence

Threats

- Most stores in the EU, therefore affected by slow growth of the EU
- Competition from other chains e.g. H&M, Zara, Matalan
- Lingering suspicion of poor working conditions amongst some suppliers

This is not a full list by any means but it does set out Primark's position in a straightforward way. It provides a starting point on which to base further and more detailed analysis.

Discussion points

Why would having most stores located within the EU be regarded as both a weakness and a threat?

Which strengths would encourage the strategists to consider branching out in the US?

What risks was Primark running when it opened in Boston?

When a business considers a future course of action, whether it is strategic or tactical, it can face a bewildering amount of information and choices. Managers will use a variety of analytical devices or tools to help them think clearly about the problems and options. One of these is SWOT analysis. SWOT is an acronym that stands for:

Strengths, **W**eaknesses, **O**pportunities, **T**hreats = **SWOT**

SWOT has been around since the '60s, primarily as a business tool but more recently it has been used to aid personal development. A SWOT analysis helps you to organise information, to analyse critical success factors and to see the bigger picture. You can identify problems and solutions and the plans you might put into place to get the most out of the future.

Think!

You could conduct a SWOT analysis on yourself by asking some questions and jotting down your answers in four separate boxes. Think about your school career and future plans...

● What are your strengths? You might be good at meeting deadlines, or writing essays, or have a positive approach to life.

● What are your weaknesses? You might not organise your notes very well, or you may find calculations difficult, or you may not be punctual.

● What opportunities are there? You may be looking at a university place or a job and where this may lead to in the future.

● What threats might you face? You may face the distractions of a too-busy social life, or the demands of a part-time job.

Internal and external factors

Strengths and Weaknesses are *internal* factors; they describe attributes that the business has within itself already. Think about your answers to these two points in the exercise you have just done.

Opportunities and Threats are *external* factors; they are dictated by circumstances that happen in the business environment and are mostly beyond its control. Again, think of your own circumstances. SWOT is often presented as a four square matrix...

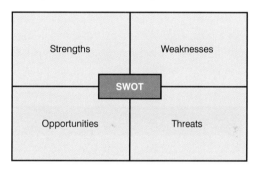

SWOT analysis involves the assessment of a product or an organisation in terms of strengths, weaknesses, opportunities and threats. Reviewing Strengths and Weaknesses allows the business to address current issues while Opportunities and Threats point the way towards future developments.

Strategic planning

In a business context, SWOT analysis is used during the early stages of strategic planning. It enables organisations to identify internal and external influences that will affect the business in both positive and negative ways. It involves a careful look at the current position of the business, prior to identifying and planning future action. The relative importance of each contributing factor can be considered, helping to reach an informed decision as to which strategy should be adopted.

In the Primark case, the company considered its critical success factors, its ability to produce popular designs at very low cost and to adjust rapidly to changing fashions. It had probably got close to market saturation in the EU and wanted to grow by diversifying into new markets. It accepted that there were elements of risk in its strategy. Dynamic markets can always throw up unexpected changes.

Not all businesses are like Primark. Analysing the way SWOT would work in a wide range of businesses requires knowledge of a whole range of relevant factors covering very different situations.

Strengths

These are things that the business does well and which are advantageous. They could include a strong market share, readily available finance, a skilled and flexible workforce, mass recognition of one or more brand names, new product development or extension strategies, perhaps led by active research and development (R&D), a reputation for reliability or good customer service, patents, customer loyalty, a track record of success.

Weaknesses

Ineffective management

These attributes could cause problems or disadvantages if they are not addressed. They could include ineffective management, difficulty in recruiting people with skills or talent, cash flow problems, low levels of retained profit, weaknesses in product design, a rarely recognised brand image, declining sales or market share, a limited range of markets or products, slowness in adopting new technologies that cut costs. Responses to known weaknesses will probably require both strategic and tactical decisions.

> **Think!**
> Which of the strengths and weaknesses would be applicable to a small business? Think of a small or medium-sized enterprise (SME) that you know and identify its strengths and weaknesses.

Opportunities

New technologies

These are areas that the business could take advantage of in the future by utilising its strengths, addressing its weaknesses or a combination of both. They could include emerging markets, new technologies, development of new market segments, a rival experiencing problems, opportunities to take over other businesses, collaboration with other organisations.

Threats

Government intervention

These are areas that are likely to have a negative impact on the business unless preventive action is taken. They come from a range of sources such as the actions of competitors, changes in consumer preferences, government intervention in the market or the economy, new regulations or industry-wide codes of conduct, available new technologies that require larger scale production, exchange rate changes, political and societal change, threats of violence.

> **WATCH OUT!**
>
> It is important to remember that what might be a strength for one business, such as the workforce or a brand name, could be a weakness in another. An opportunity for one business could also be a threat to another, such as a change in consumer preferences.

> **Exam style question**
>
> **Tesco**
>
> Tesco is one of the world's largest retailers, employing more than 500,000 people in 12 countries and serving millions of customers a week in its stores and via online shopping which is an expanding market segment. In 2015 in the UK, it still held the largest market share with 28.5%, its lowest figure in 10 years.
>
> The entire British grocery market was continuing to register 'sluggish growth'. This was due to falling prices and changing shopping habits. People were dispensing with the big weekly shop and buying goods as and when they needed them. Budget retailers were slowly chipping away at the market share of their bigger rivals. In 2015 Aldi increased sales by 18%, while Lidl increased by 12.5%. In early 2016, Amazon announced it was entering the British fresh food market via a deal with Morrison's, one of Tesco's main rivals.
>
> In Europe, Tesco's biggest sales increase of 7% was in Turkey, sales also grew in Hungary and the Czech Republic but fell by 2.8% and 1.4% in Slovakia and Poland. In Asia, restrictions on store opening hours in Korea, political instability in Thailand and economic problems in Malaysia resulted in Tesco's sales falling by at least 4% in each of those countries. Despite this the Asian division still made £565m of operating profit, more than the UK, despite a much smaller turnover.
>
> 1. Produce a SWOT analysis for Tesco based on the extract above.   (6 marks)
> 2. Assess the usefulness of a SWOT analysis for a business such as Tesco.   (8 marks)
> 3. Based on your SWOT analysis, assess two strategies that might help Tesco.   (10 marks)

Chapter 4

The impact of external influences

Challenger banks

After the financial crisis (2008-9), many said that the banks were too big to fail. As the economy recovered, the Treasury and the Bank of England encouraged small, new 'challenger' banks to enter the market. The plan was to give customers more choice and to create stronger competition in the banking sector. Metro Bank, which now has 36 branches in London, and other smaller start-ups, have benefited from their newness; they have not mis-sold pensions so people may trust them more. Also they have up to date technology platforms that are likely to be more efficient than those of some established banks.

Discussion points

What was the key change that made it possible for new small banks to get started?

Why is it reasonable to expect that at least some of them will be successful in the future?

How would you expect long-established banks to react to the newcomers?

PESTLE analysis

The PESTLE acronym stands for...

Political, **E**conomic, **S**ocial, **T**echnical, **L**egal and **E**nvironmental

This is another analytical tool, designed to make a business think more carefully about its external environment and all the factors, both local and global, that might affect it. It is sometimes known by its shorter title of PEST. The findings from PESTLE can be used to help with a SWOT analysis.

Rather like SWOT, PESTLE is a framework which leads managers to consider six areas *outside* the business that are likely to have an impact *inside* the business. The idea is then to use that information to aid strategic decision-making. But a business will not conduct a PESTLE analysis just once and then forget about it. It is an ongoing process because PESTLE factors are constantly changing and evolving.

The theory is that if the business is able to survey its current environment and assess potential changes, it will be better able than its competitors to respond to and deal with those changes. This should reduce risk. PESTLE can also be used to review a new idea or proposition, and changes in the direction of a company.

Although PESTLE is split into six headings they often intertwine and cross boundaries. For example EU regulations involve political, economic and legal issues. The rise of the digital economy is led by technological change but has economic and social consequences as well.

> **PESTLE analysis** identifies external factors that could affect the business but are actually beyond its control.

The business environment

Political factors

Government intervention

Political forces affect the business environment. Governments intervene in the economy all the time and their political leanings influence their policies. Some governments are more in favour of government intervention than others; some are more in favour of free trade while others favour less government interference and lower taxes. It is not just national governments that have an impact; what happens in other countries is also important. A new president in the White House, a change in the leadership of China and turmoil in the Middle East can all affect business operations and plans.

Political factors are intertwined with legal ones; after all, politicians enact laws and regulations, deciding on tax rates and the terms and conditions under which business operates. The difference is that political factors are shaped by attitudes, beliefs and approaches, whereas legal factors are those that have become law and must be complied with. Political viewpoints may involve influences, restrictions or opportunities, but unlike laws, they cannot compel businesses to change.

Economic factors

Oil prices

These affect the wider economy. Variables such as the level of unemployment, the rate of inflation, the stage of the business cycle, the level of government spending, interest rates and exchange rates are all wide reaching influences on business. Changes in commodity prices, particularly the price of oil, metals and energy affect businesses directly and indirectly.

> **Example**
> Much of America's recent economic recovery has been put down to the development of the shale oil and gas industry and the subsequent fall in energy costs.

On a smaller scale the level of skills, wage patterns, consumer preferences, expectations and confidence can all have an impact. Many economic variables are of course influenced by other aspects of PESTLE; political decisions change the macro economy, social changes such as immigration affect the supply and cost of labour and technological change has an impact on costs, employment and the ability of the economy to supply goods. Economic, political and technical factors favoured the challenger banks.

Social change

Migration

Societies do not stand still; as they change so too does their impact on business. Demographic changes will alter the way the population is made up and the pattern of demand. The UK population is growing, with increasing numbers of elderly and young children. This has implications for businesses that may target these market segments. Immigration is altering the size of the working population and that has an impact on employment and wage-rates.

Social trends also matter, changing attitudes to race, religion and sexuality all alter the way our society operates. There have been changes in lifestyles; people are living longer and while some trends may be decreasing such as smoking, others such as obesity are increasing. The numbers in education have risen over the last few decades, changing standards and expectations. We have seen the decline in manual occupations and the rise of the knowledge economy.

Technological change

Digital technology

Technological factors cover new inventions and developments, changes in communication and technologies, changes in the internet, e-commerce and government spending on research. This is probably the fastest growing area; some specific industries have seen rapid and far reaching changes. Digital technology has transformed the way we communicate and also the way we consume. Think about the changes in entertainment, particularly music and film and the way we shop and organise our leisure time.

Although it is often the digital and internet-related areas that grab the headlines there are many other far-reaching technological changes taking place. Materials development, new methods of manufacture, distribution and logistics, all affect the way some businesses operate. Businesses that fail to keep up to date with the latest developments run the risk of being left behind and losing sales. Several decades ago that happened to the British car industry; in more recent years Blackberry and Nokia were overtaken by Apple and Samsung.

Businesses that fail to keep up to date with the latest developments run the risk of being left behind.

Legal

Regulation

All businesses have to operate within a legal framework that includes all the laws, rules and regulations that must be complied with. Businesses must consider existing legal requirements and any planned ones. Those that trade overseas need to be aware of any differences in the legal code of their target markets, compared to their home market. Businesses need to know what is and what is not legal in order to trade successfully. Tariffs may make exports less competitive.

> **Examples** might include, national employment laws, minimum wage legislation, international trade regulations and restrictions, competition law, consumer protection, health and safety, equal opportunities, advertising standards, product labeling and product safety.

Environmental

Waste disposal

Some natural resources are finite in quantity; there is a growing environmental awareness of the need to conserve them and to follow sustainable practices. Waste disposal and recycling procedures are now much more important; many were driven by legal requirements. For example in the EU all electrical equipment retailers have to pay a levy that goes towards recycling electrical equipment.

Having a responsible environmental policy is increasingly important, partly due to consumer pressure but also because it is seen as the right thing to do. For example, Marks & Spencer introduced its 'Plan A' – *"Plan A is our way to help protect the planet – by sourcing responsibly, reducing waste and helping communities."*

Apple – a PESTLE analysis

New technologies

P
- Apple manufactures in China and is therefore dependent on stability in China. Future political unrest could be disruptive.
- Apple is under pressure to bring at least some production back to the USA (reshoring).
- Some American politicians are urging tariffs and sanctions on imports from China.

E
- Despite Apple's strong brand image it is estimated that sales revenue in the EU was 16% lower because of the 2008-12 recession and economic downturn.
- Wage levels are rising in China, increasing manufacturing costs.
- The dollar is currently (2016) strong in relation to the pound, euro and many other currencies.

S
- For Apple to continue to grow it needs to enter emerging markets where the brand does not have the loyalty and appeal it has in western markets.
- There are continuing ethical concerns about Apple's manufacturing in China, despite recent reforms.

T
- Technological advances by rivals mean that many Apple features are no longer unique.
- Growing availability and use of smartphones and tablets may reduce demand for Apple's computers.
- Growing capabilities of fraudsters make Apple products more vulnerable.

L
- Apple pay and its interest in developing an 'Apple car' mean entering new areas with high levels of regulation.
- Apple relies on protecting its intellectual property rights and may need to fight more legal battles (as with Samsung) as new rivals enter the market.

E
- Apple is already running a re-cycling programme for its products but may have to do more.
- China's attempts to reduce pollution and greenhouse gases may have an impact on Apple's manufacturing base.

The changing competitive environment

The competitive environment is constantly changing. It is dynamic and a business that fails to take this into account runs a considerable risk of losing market share and ultimately, closing down. The competitive environment involves direct and indirect competitors. PESTLE factors can change that environment.

Direct competitors – in a healthy market with lots of competition a business will have direct rivals who produce very similar products and services, McDonalds competes directly with Burger King, Barclays with HSBC, Asda with Tesco and so on. A consumer can choose between them.

Direct rivals

Indirect competitors – are not direct rivals in the same type of business but they are competing for the same consumer spending power. A consumer who has bought a new fitted kitchen may have decided not to buy a new car. The kitchen provider and the car showroom are in indirect competition for that consumer's spending power. Similarly, the supermarket selling ready meals competes with the local takeaway.

Market structures

- Very **competitive markets** may have many competing businesses, all offering similar products. In an open market there may be five stalls selling cauliflowers that all look fresh and appetising. Prices will have to be very similar; charging a higher price will mean selling none.

- A **monopolist**, a single business with no competitors, will be able to choose the price.

- In between are many businesses that compete on design, appearance, practicality, value for money and many other factors. Product differentiation will be important because it will enable the business to charge more and generate profit; the same applies to other marketing activities.

PESTLE factors will affect market structures in a range of ways. Around the areas of direct and indirect competition, they will influence the competitive environment and create a process of constant change. For example:

CMA

- The **Competition and Markets Authority** (**CMA**) is a government body that acts as a watchdog, investigating anti-competitive practices and imposing heavy penalties on businesses that act illegally. For example, forming a cartel, a group of businesses that agree to fix prices, is illegal. The CMA can protect consumers from fraudulent business practices.

- The **growth of international trade** means that many markets are very much more competitive than they were in the past. This forces many businesses to strive for greater efficiency, cutting costs and improving product features.

- **New technologies** facilitate the development of new products, new designs and cheaper production methods. The new products and reduced production costs and prices change the competitive environment.

- Businesses that cannot keep up with changing **environmental regulations** will have little chance of competing and staying in business.

> **Show your understanding**
> 1. Research and compile a PESTLE analysis for Tesco.
> 2. Now go back and look at your SWOT analysis from the last chapter. Is there anything extra that you can now add?
> 3. Does this change your recommendations for possible strategies? If so why?

Porter's five forces

Michael Porter set out his ideas in 1980 in his book 'Competitive Strategy'. Put simply, he described five forces that determined where power lay in a given market situation. These five forces look at how constant change influences a business, helping it to understand both the strength of the current competitive position, and the strength of a position it might consider for the future.

Once a business knows where power lies it can exploit a situation of strength, improve a situation of weakness, and avoid mistakes. The five forces can help the business to decide whether new products or services have the potential to be profitable.

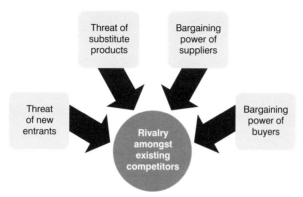

Rivalry amongst existing competitors

For Porter, this is the most important area and the main force determining the ability of a business to influence its market. The more competitors that there are, the more competitive the market is and the less influence each business has over its rivals. Think about individual farmers who have little or no control over the prices they receive for their produce. Markets that have only a few competing firms are rather less competitive and each individual business has some control. Think of large supermarkets and banks.

Even if there are many competitors and the market is competitive, a business can gain influence if it is able to *differentiate* itself in some way. This could involve a brand name or an innovation; in the mind of the consumer there will be fewer substitutes, making it easier to compete. In this way, the small delicatessen selling local and organic produce is able to compete successfully against the big food retailers.

If the market is expanding rapidly, competition may be less fierce; there is room for all to increase output and individual businesses will have more influence in the market. The opposite is also true, as markets slow and even begin to shrink, competition intensifies and it becomes harder just to survive.

The threat of new entrants

If it is easy for new businesses to enter the market then competition is likely to be greater. The ability to do so is governed by the presence or otherwise of *barriers to entry*. These can take many forms such as start-up costs, the need for economies of scale (see pages 21-23) or having to compete against established brand names. They all increase start-up costs, restricting the ability of businesses to enter the market and thus decreasing competition.

The threat of substitute products

Products that are similar, with little differentiation, are likely to face more competition because in the mind of the consumer there is little to choose between them. This restricts the power of the individual business to raise price and reduces its influence in the market. This is why businesses go to so much trouble to differentiate their products and to advertise.

The bargaining power of suppliers

Much depends on the number of suppliers and the type of product or service they supply. If there are many suppliers all selling similar things then the business has much more choice. This gives the business more power in the relationship, especially if the cost of switching suppliers is low and they can drive down the cost of supplies by threatening to go elsewhere. If there is a limited number of suppliers (or even just one) then the power lies with the supplier. Think of Microsoft and PC manufacturers.

Competition

Differentiation

Barriers
to entry

Assessing proposals

Market power

The bargaining power of buyers

A similar argument applies to buyers. When there are only a few, they have much greater power and control over the prices they are prepared to pay. Big supermarkets such as Tesco are often accused of treating their suppliers badly by imposing harsh trading terms and by driving down prices. When there are many buyers the opposite is true.

By conducting an analysis using Porter's five forces a business can make a judgement as to whether or not entering a new market may be viable. Profitable industries are likely to have relatively weak suppliers and buyers, high barriers to entry, few substitutes and low levels of rivalry. Less profitable industries are likely to have relatively strong suppliers and buyers, low barriers to entry, many substitutes and high levels of rivalry.

Example – Starbucks: Porter's five forces analysis

Threat of new entrants	Threat of substitute products	Rivalry amongst competitors	Bargaining power of suppliers	Bargaining power of buyers
LOW – the market is already saturated; new entrants would need to fund substantial amounts of investment to compete on the same scale and against the brand name.	**LOW** – It could be argued that other drinks such as tea, juices and soft drinks are substitutes but for many coffee drinkers they are not close substitutes.	**HIGH** – Starbucks operates in a competitive industry with major competitors like Costa, McDonald's, Caffé Nero and thousands of small local coffee shops and cafes.	**LOW** (but increasing) – many global coffee producers to choose from but as the trend for organic or fair trade coffee increases, suppliers are fewer and more organised.	**MEDIUM** – individual customer power is low but it is easy for them to move to a rival particularly if an effective marketing campaign or loyalty scheme is used.

Exam style questions

1. Using the example above comment on the degree of market power that Starbucks has. *(4 marks)*

2. Complete a five forces analysis for Apple or any other business of your choosing. *(8 marks)*

3. Evaluate the usefulness of Porter's five forces analysis and other decision making tools to a business such as Apple. *(12 marks)*

Chapter 5

Growth

Airbus

The UK has traditionally been very active in aircraft design and production. In 1959, UK aircraft manufacturers had already planned a new approach to air travel and called it Airbus. But the market was dominated by the big US manufacturers, primarily Boeing. Furthermore, any UK development would face competition from French and German companies. In fact, all the European companies were in the same boat – each one knew that current sales levels and profits were too low to finance the development of a big new aircraft. They began to collaborate.

Within the UK, France and Germany, separate businesses merged. In the UK a number of businesses combined to form BAE Systems, creating an organisation that could undertake major research and development projects. BAE collaborated with other European firms to create Airbus Industrie, which is strong enough to compete with Boeing in the cutthroat market for passenger aircraft. It now employs 63,000 people in France, Germany, Spain, China and the UK. Together, they reap economies of scale. To cut costs, they had to grow bigger.

Designers and engineers work on fuel systems, landing gear and aerodynamic research at Filton near Bristol. The wings for the A380 (and other models) are made at Broughton near Chester. The wings are taken by road and then river to a specially designed roll-on-roll-off ferry that takes them to France; the Airbus is assembled at Toulouse.

This long standing European collaboration has deprived Boeing of a monopoly. The competition forces both manufacturers to maximise efficiency and innovation and has helped to cut the real costs of air travel.

Discussion points

Why was it impossible for independent aircraft manufacturers to develop new aircraft?

What had to happen in order to make the Airbus range so successful?

Revise: Businesses have many reasons for wanting to grow. Some of these figured in your work on business objectives in Theme 1, Section 1.5.3; revising the key terms will be helpful as a basis for this chapter. Also, make sure you understand capacity utilisation. Chapter 2 (pages 5-8) covers corporate strategy which is often concerned with growth.

Objectives of growth

Cost efficiency

Key reasons for a business to plan for growth are profit maximisation, sales maximisation and increasing market share. All of these are likely to require increased output. All will work best when the business is looking at strategies for competing effectively. These would typically involve both price and non-price competition. But whatever the favoured strategy, cost cutting is going to be important. Cutting costs with no change in price enhances profit. Cutting costs and prices usually makes it possible to increase sales. Cost efficiency frequently involves looking for economies of scale.

Economies of scale

Business growth can lead to economies of scale in a whole range of ways. Equally, economies of scale can make business growth easier. As the business increases its output, total costs are likely to rise. **Internal economies of scale** are achieved within each individual business. **External economies** benefit the whole industry. The objective is always to reduce average total costs in order to gain a competitive advantage. Businesses that can't cut costs, when their competitors do, will have to diversify or close down.

Economies of scale

Where there are high fixed costs of design and development, output has to be high in order to spread the cost. Sometimes mergers are required so that market share can be increased and output can grow enough to make the development process worthwhile. Airbus increased market share by collaboration rather than merger, creating a company that could afford to spend heavily on design and development in order to build better aircraft.

> **Economies of scale** include all the ways in which long run increases in capacity and output can reduce average costs.
>
> **Internal economies of scale** arise when a business invests in expanding production.
>
> **External economies** involve unit cost reductions that are shared by a whole industry, rather than a single business. External economies are common when many businesses are concentrated in one location, because there will be a pool of appropriately skilled labour and local suppliers.

Internal economies

Spare capacity

Utilising spare capacity works when a business finds demand for its products increasing. If their equipment is idle some of the time, selling more might enable them to make full use of the spare capacity, just by using it more. The production costs would increase with the number of employees required and the other extra inputs, but the fixed costs would stay the same and would be spread more thinly across the increased output. Unit costs (i.e. average total costs) would fall.

> **Example**
> This happened at Jaguar Land Rover in 2012-13. Demand for their vehicles was rising in China; this enabled them to run an extra shift, using the same assembly line twice over each day instead of just once. Profits increased.

Technical economies are particularly relevant in manufacturing, construction and transport. A bigger ocean going tanker with double the capacity will not need double the crew. However, expensive specialist machinery is only worthwhile if kept busy.

> **Example**
> Car body panels can be produced in seconds by giant presses costing millions of pounds each. Such specialist machinery is a fundamental part of mass production. But it is only worthwhile where the market size for each machine will justify the expense, or where the machines can easily switch between design specifications.

Marketing economies involve advertising and promotion activities. Making an advert is a fixed cost which will not change as output increases. Spreading fixed costs across more units of production reduces average cost. Once a business is large enough to operate nationally, mass media such as newspapers and commercial television become more effective. Coca-Cola can use the same advertisements, with different voiceovers, in many countries.

Human capital

Managerial economies focus on having specialists in management roles. As business size increases, it pays to use specialists. For example, accountants, human resource managers and marketing experts can be recruited. Their specialist input should improve the team's performance. This is human capital.

Other economies of scale include financial, bulk-buying and risk-bearing economies. *Financial economies* arise when banks see larger firms as more secure so charge lower rates of interest. *Bulk-buying* allows larger firms to negotiate cheaper input costs, as seen with UK supermarkets. *Risk-bearing economies* are achieved when firms diversify; failed innovations can be offset against profits from successful projects. Mars, Cadbury or Nestlé can launch new chocolate bars frequently, knowing that some will fail but others will be profitable.

Show your understanding

Unilever produces 400 different brands, produced and sold almost all over the world, for example Dove, Flora and Knorr. Its strapline is 'On any given day, two billion people use Unilever products to look good, feel good and get more out of life'.

Identify specific internal economies of scale that could have contributed to their growth, explaining each one.

External economies come into play when the whole industry is growing. They are particularly important when the industry is concentrated in one area. Specialist suppliers and support industries develop. Car component suppliers are found around car assembly plants, for example. Businesses and local training providers can develop a pool of labour with the right skills. Technical colleges in most areas train workers for major local industries. Universities may get involved in relevant research.

External economies benefit all the firms in an industry, reducing their costs. They do not give an individual firm an advantage over local competitors who share the cost savings. However, businesses that benefit from external economies can gain a considerable advantage over foreign rivals.

Minimum efficient scale

Economies of scale will push average costs down as output increases, giving larger businesses a competitive advantage. They might charge similar prices but use some of the extra revenue for research and development that generates innovations. The lowest level of output at which the lowest average cost is reached is known as the **minimum efficient scale**. Businesses that are smaller than the minimum efficient scale have a cost disadvantage. In the past, new technologies have almost always raised the output level of the minimum efficient scale. This may be changing. Some new technologies – e.g. 3D printing – may reduce the minimum efficient scale.

An industry may have many competing businesses, all able to reach minimum efficient scale. (This often occurs in the service sector.) But sometimes, available economies of scale are so great that there is only enough demand for a few firms. Global demand for large commercial aircraft is such that only Boeing and Airbus compete in their production.

Minimum efficient scale is the lowest level of output at which average or unit costs are minimised.

Increased market power

Where there are many businesses competing with each other, each business has to operate as efficiently as possible and accept the going market price. This is attractive for customers. It is less attractive for businesses as it leaves little scope for increasing profits. Some may have to be happy aiming for survival.

The possibility of developing market power creates an incentive for many businesses to grow. In markets that are dominated by a few large businesses, each one will have some market power. This can be deployed in many ways.

- Product differentiation and branding may make some products distinctive enough for customers to choose them in preference to a cheaper alternative.

- Product reputation or reliability or good customer service may attract customers who will pay more for better quality.

- Some businesses rely entirely on non-price competition; this can mean that all of them are setting prices above the minimum possible and consumers have no choice but to accept those prices.

- At the extreme, a pure monopoly has just one supplier with no competition; it can profit from raising prices and is under little pressure to operate efficiently.

External economies

Strong competition

Branding

Market power

Example

The rapid growth of Sky TV subscriptions in the UK was partly due to its monopoly over live broadcasting rights for many major sporting events. Sky now has 12 million UK subscribers and made £675m profits in the second half of 2014.

Think!

If you fly abroad, look at the price of bottled water in airport terminal shops. Passengers can't take their own drinks through security and the shops have market power. Prices can be much higher than outside the airport where there is more competition. Think of another example of market power.

Some businesses have power over suppliers because of their market share. Small suppliers who depend on big buyers are in a very weak bargaining position. Many farmers complain that the leading supermarkets use their power to reduce prices and impose unreasonable conditions, such as delaying payments.

Market share and brand recognition

Choosing your toilet roll

There are marked variations in the types of toilet roll bought in different countries. In many EU countries consumers buy mainly own label and economy rolls. These take two thirds of sales in Germany, for example. British consumers prefer branding, luxury and softness. Andrex is the leading brand with roughly 30% of the market; Cushelle, Charmin and Velvet also sell well; this is described as a highly competitive market.

In 2011, Kimberly-Clark, which owns Andrex, detected signs of trouble ahead. Their market research told them that brand loyalty was waning. They hired consultants to advise; the result was a rebrand and packaging re-design. The idea was to *"deflect attention from price to value."* They reached for the puppy again. In the words of the designers *"The puppy was key to emotionally re-engaging with consumers… With his head tilted at a disarming angle… he engages directly, making an emotional plea that is difficult to ignore."* It worked. Market share went up by 15% in 2012.

Marketing strategies

Think!

The marketing budget for this exercise would have been expensive, involving extensive market research and advertising. Why was it worth it?

What does this tell you about consumers?

Many businesses have strong and established brands. If you travel to a different town and want to buy a coffee, you will have choices. A small local coffee shop might offer high quality coffee and attentive service. Experimenting is low risk; the worst outcome is a poor cup of coffee. However, many people see Costa, Starbucks or Café Nero as reassuringly predictable. Even with relatively high prices, these three combined have around a 75% UK market share.

Having a significant market share makes **brand recognition** easier to achieve. It is an important way of differentiating products from competitors. A strong, recognised brand is a valuable asset. Many consumers will pay high prices for the best-known brands. Business growth increases brand recognition; equally, it is easier to maintain and increase market share with a strong brand.

> **Brand recognition** measures the percentage of consumers who recognise a specific brand and associate it with product features. A high percentage makes branding a valuable marketing tool.

Branding is often used as a way to charge higher prices.

Increasing profitability

Profit

Branding is often used as a way to charge higher prices. But there are fine choices to be made as to how profits can be increased. Avoiding big price increases and giving good value for money can be excellent ways to make a profit. (Think of John Lewis, which stayed profitable all through the recession, 2008-12, even when other businesses were struggling.) If sales are really strong, profits can be made even with wafer-thin profit margins. A major supermarket might make just a penny or two on each container of milk sold, but millions of people buy milk regularly so the pennies add up. Growing bigger and selling more benefits businesses.

The simple point here is that growth and increasing sales volume raise profits. The eMarketer estimate is that 1.9 billion smartphones are in use globally in 2015, with roughly half of them using the Android operating system. In addition to its value to Google (owner of Android), this creates attractive potential profits for developers of 'apps' for Android.

Diseconomies of scale

Bigger is not always better. Economies of scale, market power, strong brands and increasing volume of business can be linked to growth of a business, profit and success. But beyond a certain point, increasing size may bring disadvantages rather than advantages, pushing average costs up.

Co-ordination problems

Decision-taking involves collaboration between many departments and individuals. There is a need for effective delegation. Keeping different parts of the production process efficiently co-ordinated may get harder. The number of people to be involved or consulted can grow to the point where meetings are uncomfortably large. Contacts inevitably become less personal. There is an increasing chance of conflicting decisions in different departments

The business may become less flexible, less able to respond swiftly to market changes. Employees may feel distant from management in a large organisation and may feel de-motivated. Some smaller businesses want to grow; many others have good reasons for staying as they are.

Diseconomies of scale

These disadvantages are sources of **diseconomies of scale**. Where diseconomies can arise at relatively low levels of output, as in many personal services, the optimum size of business will be relatively small. For example, personal trust and understanding matter to many hairdressing salons. There are chains, but independent salons thrive because of strong relationships with customers. This can bring steady repeat business, reducing the need for expensive marketing.

> **Diseconomies of scale** increase unit costs as a business grows. They are often associated with communication issues or costs of co-ordination.

Figure 5.1 illustrates economies and diseconomies of scale. The vast majority of businesses find economies of scale at some stage in their development, before they reach their minimum efficient scale. Then many will find that they can expand without costs rising; this is the flat-bottomed part of the U-shaped cost curve. Growing further, businesses meet diseconomies of scale. In reality, the curve is unlikely to be so even. Diseconomies of scale will usually be smaller than earlier economies.

Figure 5.1: Economies and diseconomies of scale

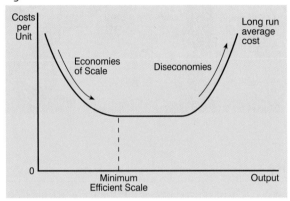

> **Think!**
> Marks & Spencer grew very fast for a long time but then faced recurring problems of profitability. Why might this be?

Overtrading

Growing too fast

Sometimes a business grows very fast. A good idea can lead to fast-rising demand. Just offering good value for money can attract many customers. These businesses can encounter diseconomies of scale, not because growing larger causes long-term problems, but because they do not have enough working capital to cover their short-run costs. Consequently they run into cash-flow problems. This is especially likely if there is a long gap between doing the work and receiving payment. Having to offer trade credit can make matters worse.

A particular problem is that rapid growth requires investment in additional capacity and with weak cash flow this will be almost impossible. Many new businesses find that they cannot continue because of lack of cash, even though in the long run the business is likely to be profitable.

Growth

Ardagh's bottles

Ardagh, started up in the Republic of Ireland in 1932 as a small-time manufacturer of glass bottles. In 1998 the strategy changed to one of growth via acquisition which included buying up bottle makers in the EU, North America and elsewhere. The company now provides packaging containers of all kinds including a metals division which specialises in drink and food cans. This strategy made a lot of sense. Glass was becoming less popular as packaging shifted towards lower cost materials. Customers include Coca-Cola, Heineken, John West and Proctor and Gamble.

In 1998 Paul Coulson became company Chairman; he has a substantial personal holding in the company. He has shown phenomenal skills in raising the finance needed to expand the company, including running investor roadshows in financial centres and borrowing on the international bond market. He managed to raise the finance needed for expansion even when the banking system was in crisis between 2010 and 2013.

Paul Coulson, Chairman of Ardagh.

As well as moving into international markets, Coulson has diversified the company's product line. One of his most striking acquisitions was Impress Group, a metal container specialist bought for €1.7 billion in 2010. In 2012 Ardagh bought Anchor Glass in the USA for $880m. Anchor had been close to bankruptcy but Ardagh made it into a big player. In 2013 the company acquired St.Gobain's Verallia North America for €1.3 billion. The company is now based in Luxembourg. It has 19,000 employees spread over 89 production sites (down from 100 in 2013).

Questions
1. Explain how the growth strategy allowed Ardagh to diversify.
2. Should Ardagh integrate the management of the different companies or allow separate areas to function independently? Outline the advantages and disadvantages of each approach.

Taking precautions

When looking at mergers and takeovers, it is crucial to examine the difference between the aims and expectations of the merger, and the actual results. No business enters into a merger with the expectation that it will fail, but statistics show the reality is very different. The reasons for failure vary: a clash of **corporate cultures** caused the failure of the 1998 merger between Daimler-Benz and Chrysler. Problems relating to a lack of **due diligence** occurred when RBS bought Dutch bank ABN AMRO. Ardagh probably took great care to investigate the businesses they have taken over before coming to a decision.

> **Corporate cultures** grow from the shared values, attitudes, standards and beliefs that characterise an organisation and define its nature.
>
> **Due diligence** refers to the careful investigations that should take place when major transactions may be affected by the financial or legal situation of the companies concerned.

Why do mergers and takeovers happen?

Mergers

Example – Merger activity in the pharmaceutical industry

The pharmaceutical industry is one sector which shows almost continual merger and acquisition activity, partially because the huge sums needed to take products from the R&D stage to the market mean smaller firms simply do not have the resources. Add to that the huge rewards of a successful launch and it is easy to see why businesses that may have legally protected a new development by patenting are suddenly very attractive. In 2011 the four biggest mergers in the industry alone were valued at over $75 billion. At the same time firms are selling off slower areas of their business, resulting in an industry where companies combine, split and recombine in different ways at breakneck speed. The 2011 figure is now being dwarfed. In the first half of 2015 alone $221 billion of pharmaceutical deals were made.

Discussion point

Given that so many businesses in this industry change rapidly, is it possible that corporate culture no longer matters so much?

It is worth looking at the motives behind a merger or a takeover. Was it an aggressive strategy to eliminate competition, or an ambitious move to enter new markets? Was it a strategy of diversification, designed to reduce risk? (Think of Ansoff's Matrix.) Was the reason to gain competitive advantage through access to new technology or was it simply a better alternative to organic growth (growing internally, which takes longer)? These reasons can be broken down into strategic, financial and tactical reasons.

Competitive advantage

Strategic reasons are those that aim to improve the business and gain some aspect of competitive advantage. This does not necessarily imply growth. It could be a defensive strategy to consolidate a position. These were clearly visible in many pharmaceutical mergers and acquisitions.

Financial reasons are often driven by the desire to maximise shareholder wealth and therefore the overriding factor will be the expected impact on future financial performance.

Managerial reasons focus on the personal intentions of managers. There may be a clash here with shareholders. If a business is pursuing a strategy of long term growth via acquisitions, which may require finance through borrowing, then the directors will need to convince shareholders that a short term sacrifice will be beneficial in the long run.

Within these three main reasons for mergers and acquisitions there will be a whole range of other motives, and in reality the merger will be driven by a many different factors.

Merger	Reason
Santander / Abbey	Access to the UK market
British Airways / Iberia	Economies of scale, defence against economic downturn
Kraft / Cadbury	Global growth strategy
Tata / JLR	Access to emerging markets, diversification
RBS / ABN AMRO	Reputation, market dominance, personal goals
Nestlé / Rowntree	Market share (particularly KitKat)
Ladbrokes / Coral	Defence against new entrants
Ardagh / Anchor Glass	Increasing value by better management

Controversially, it may suggest that the fewer firms there are in an industry, the more efficient the industry becomes (because there is less duplication for the consumer). When T-Mobile merged with Orange in the UK, they said *"The ambition is to combine both the Orange and T-Mobile networks, cut out duplication, and create a single super-network. For customers it will mean a bigger network and better coverage, while reducing the number of stations and sites, which is good for cost reduction as well as being good for the environment."*

The distinction between mergers and takeovers

Cultural identity

The Battle for Cadbury

In 2010, American giant Kraft finally secured the takeover of UK icon Cadbury for £11.5 billion but the process was not a smooth one. With Cadbury seen as a traditional UK brand, many investors were concerned about losing its cultural identity, but the final price was too high to ignore.

August 2009: Irene Rosenfeld, CEO of Kraft met with Roger Carr, Chairman of Cadbury to outline a takeover deal. Shareholders would be offered 300p in cash and 0.2589 of new Kraft shares for each share in Cadbury. This valued Cadbury shares at 755p each. In September Kraft publicly announced the bid, but by this time the value had slipped a little, valuing Cadbury at £10.2bn. Cadbury shareholders rejected the bid and asked the UK Takeover Panel to request that a 'put up or shut up' order be sent to Kraft. This formalises a time frame for any takeover. The UK takeover panel ruled that Kraft had until 5pm on 9th November to make a formal offer, or they must withdraw their interest in the company for six months.

November 2009: Kraft posts weaker than expected revenue figures. Irene Rosenfeld reiterates that she will not overpay for Cadbury. By 9th November Kraft had formalised its offer for Cadbury on the same terms as before, but weaker than expected Kraft share prices meant the combined share and cash offer only valued Cadbury shares at 717p now. By mid-November separate rumours that Ferrero and Hershey were also considering a bid for Cadbury pushed the share price to 819½ pence per share.

December 2009: The defence heats up. Kraft posted its offer to Cadbury shareholders. Cadbury promised their shareholders bigger dividends and stronger growth as well as reminding them of the possibility of rival bids from Ferrero and Hershey.

January 2010: Kraft changes the terms. The overall value remains the same but Kraft offers 60p more per share and reduces the Kraft share offer. Cadbury reports good trading over the Christmas period and rejects the bid. At the same time, however, Ferrero pulls out of the running. On 19th January Kraft finally sealed the deal, paying shareholders 500p in cash and 0.1874 Kraft shares for each Cadbury share. The equivalent value of 840p per share was less than both the CEO and Chairman of Cadbury wanted.

The final deal of 840p (or equivalent) per share was 48% more than the Cadbury share price prior to Kraft's initial approach.

Source: www.telegraph.co.uk

Discussion points

1. Why do you think Kraft made a 'cash plus share' offer to existing Cadbury shareholders rather than just a simple cash offer?

2. The takeover caused significant anger about a UK business being bought out by a large American company who people thought would fundamentally alter the culture of Cadbury and cut jobs. To what extent do you agree that these concerns were justified?

Hostile takeovers

A **takeover** occurs when one business has bought over half of the shares in another business, although in reality a shareholder with significantly more shares than others tends to have more influence in Annual General Meetings and can influence the direction a business takes by voting power. Takeovers can be 'friendly' or 'hostile' depending on whether the sale is agreed by all parties. Friendly takeovers tend to happen when private limited companies or smaller businesses become amalgamated with larger firms. Hostile takeovers occur when the shares are bought on the stock exchange without the agreement of the company. This usually involves the company making the takeover paying a share price above the market price to encourage existing shareholders to sell. The target business is then either absorbed into the larger business or closed down. **Mergers** on the other hand, occur when two businesses agree to join together to form a new company, often under a new name, for example when BA merged with Iberia to become IAG.

A takeover can be hostile if the target company does not want to be taken over.

Dawn raids

> **Mergers** combine two businesses under one management, which may include individuals from both.
>
> **Takeovers** occur when one businesses buys a controlling share (i.e. 51% or more) of another business. It may be hostile or friendly.
>
> The term **M&A**, mergers and acquisitions, covers both mergers and takeovers.
>
> The world of takeovers and mergers has its own language. For example, a **dawn raid** is a type of takeover when a firm buys as many shares in a target company as possible as soon as the market opens, thereby avoiding the price hikes that come with announcing their intentions in advance. **Black knights** are companies making hostile takeovers whereas **white knights** is used to describe more friendly takeovers, and **poison pills** are attempts by the company being taken over to make their stock less attractive.

Horizontal and vertical integration

When a business either merges with or takes over a business at the same stage of production, this is known as **horizontal integration**. This is one of the most common forms of integration and allows access to potentially new and larger markets as well as benefits from economies of scale. This can be good for consumers if prices are kept low and firms can concentrate on delivering high quality products rather than needing to keep an eye on what the competition is doing. On the other hand, it does mean that the market is less competitive, which could mean consumers have less choice.

Economies of scale

Horizontal integration does not mean that a new business is automatically formed. It might be that the brands continue with very little change. For example when Nestlé bought Rowntree, they were not trying to merge the two businesses into something new, but did want the famous Rowntree brands. Doing so increased Nestlé's share of the confectionary market significantly.

Vertical integration on the other hand occurs when a business merges with or takes over another firm at a different stage of production. This can be **backward** vertical integration which occurs when one company buys a supplier, i.e. a business at a previous stage of production. For example, a furniture manufacturing

Vertical integration

company might buy a timber supplier. **Forward** vertical integration occurs when one company buys another company closer to the end user. Thinking of the same furniture company, this may mean buying a chain of retail outlets. With backward vertical integration (BVI), the firm now has access to reliable supplies of materials and, furthermore, the supplier can either sell them to competitors, thus generating revenue, or restrict supplies to give the business a competitive advantage. Similarly with forward vertical integration (FVI) the original firm now has a retail outlet for their products and can dictate that the retailer does not sell competitors' products, again giving them an advantage.

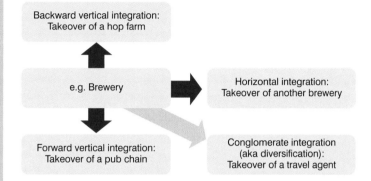

Conglomerate integration

Example

Paypal, owned by Ebay, is an online platform which allows individuals and businesses to transfer money electronically. It now has over 100 million active accounts and is used in 190 countries worldwide. In 2005 Paypal paid $370 million for VeriSign, the payment portal service. Paypal had been paying to use the service for many years and it made sense to buy it outright and therefore save money in the long run. As technology developed and the scale of digital payment increased, particularly on mobile phones, it was clear VeriSign were not providing the benefits Paypal expected. So, in 2013 they paid $800 million for Chicago-based payments gateway Braintree. The takeover is expected to provide benefits to both parties. Braintree is used by a lot of start-up tech companies such as Uber and Airbnb. CEO of Braintree, Bill Ready, said *"The alignment with Paypal means Braintree can continue to push the boundaries of innovation while expanding into new markets with increased speed and confidence."*

Financial risks and rewards

Rationalisation

It is common for a business following a strategy of acquisition to expect financial rewards. These could come from rationalisation, which means eliminating duplication in both production processes and overhead requirements. Other ways to cut costs include economies of scale that come with increased size and gains in revenue that result from reduced competition or larger markets. The notion of two businesses together having greater strength than if they were independent is known as **synergy**. The expectation is that the sum total of the merged business is greater than that of two separate companies. Put simply, it is the suggestion that $1 + 1 = 3$.

More often than not however, the reality does not meet the expectation. For example, in 2005 eBay bought Skype for $2.6 billion, only to sell them four years later for $1.9 billion. The two companies were unable to integrate their technological systems, according to PC world. Examples of financially successful mergers are rarer, but still exist. Disney Corporation has a history of successful growth through acquisition, including Marvel Comics and, more significantly, Pixar. However one of the biggest successful mergers in history took place in 1999 when Exxon and Mobil signed an $81 billion agreement to merge and form ExxonMobil, thereby forming the biggest oil company in the world.

> **Synergy** refers to the way in which two companies combined may have greater strength than they had as separate entities. They may reap economies of scale and may be able to reduce duplication of some management resources. However, synergy may fail to emerge as expected.

Problems of rapid growth

Generally speaking, growth through acquisition (inorganic growth) is quicker than organic growth and this can pose problems. (Chapter 7 has more detail on organic and inorganic growth.) Diseconomies of scale can result from problems in coordination and communication and as a business grows, it can lose focus on what it is good at (its core competency). Change can be disruptive and sometimes unpopular, and if resistance to change is not carefully managed then performance will be affected.

Poor communication

Risk

Mergers and takeovers are high risk strategies and a business must find the balance between taking too long to prepare and acting too quickly. Take too long and it signals your intentions to rival firms, possibly risking a rival bid and takeover battles. Act too quickly and you run the risk of being poorly prepared. A company should develop a clear vision as to what the merged company will stand for, how it will operate, and what benefits stakeholders can expect to see. Exactly when and to whom this message is communicated will depend on the relative importance of stakeholder groups. The business may wish to carry out stakeholder mapping, carefully planning its approach so as to ensure communication is successful.

Lack of preparation

The RBS takeover of ABN AMRO is a classic example of a firm which acted too quickly and without due diligence. Fred Goodwin, then CEO of RBS, is often seen as a case study of a leader acting for his own motives and a misguided assumption that he was unable to fail. It ended with RBS falling into public ownership. Businesses need detailed implementation plans that evaluate the extent of changes which will be made as a result of the merger.

Lack of cultural cohesion

Culture clashes

When two businesses come together, one of the biggest problems could be the clash of cultures. Corporate culture is deeply ingrained in the way a business operates; decisions concerning acquisition must be very carefully taken. Whether there is a merger or a takeover, the business must consider – should it create something new, impose one culture on another, or allow both companies to exist under the same ownership? When Daimler-Benz merged with Chrysler the cultures of a German and an American car manufacturer were simply too different, and the merger failed. Similarly when Time Warner and America Online (AOL) came together for $164 billion no-one expected the culture clash to be as big as it was. Although there were also external factors which affected the success, the companies simply could not work together and finally split in 2009. If a business is used to a certain type of leadership style or approach to decision making, then changing to a new model of organisation is likely to cause problems.

ANSWERS

Page 69, Critical path analysis

(a)

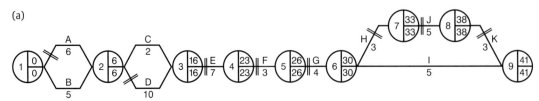

(b) critical path: A, D, E, F, G, H, J, K [– the bar marks go alongside each letter]

(c) B = 1 week, C = 8 weeks, I = 6 weeks

You might notice that in this diagram all nodes lie on the critical path so the EST and LFT figures are the same within each node. Remember that any nodes not on the critical path would have differences between the EST and LFT.

Chapter 7
Organic growth

Marks and Spencer

The original Mr Marks was a refugee who started with a market stall in 1884. It was in the early 1920s that the business really began to grow. In the UK it currently has 852 retail outlets. This growth has been almost entirely organic.

In 1973 M&S branched out internationally. Now it has 52 outlets in India and much smaller numbers in many other places. Globally, M&S has set up joint ventures and bought some local retail chains, growing by both organic and inorganic means.

Strong growth was based on being known to give value for money. That worked well for a long time. In recent years problems have arisen, particularly in relation to falling clothing sales. M&S reacted by trying to introduce new brands but this has not to date been very successful.

Discussion points

Think about the reasons why organic growth worked so well for M&S.

Consider possible reasons why M&S clothing sales growth later slowed.

What possibilities might have opened up if M&S had been prepared to consider acquiring other clothing retailers in the UK?

Achieving growth

Market share

In a growing market, sales revenue can be increased simply by producing and selling more. The business will grow even if its market share remains the same. Alternatively if the market is not growing, the business can still expand by increasing market share. Either way, the product has got to be competitive. Strategic decision-taking will have to focus on maintaining and if possible increasing competitiveness.

Marks and Spencer chose to grow organically and succeeded because of its reputation for good value. Other businesses that have done well through organic growth include Ikea and JCB. **Organic growth** means expanding internally, creating extra capacity within the business. It involves using retained profits and loan capital to increase production capacity. There will be investment in capital and more employees may be recruited, including people with specialised skills. This will lead to higher turnover (sales revenue). This can also be achieved by developing a more sophisticated product that sells at a higher price due to its quality. Energetic marketing may be significant.

> **Organic growth** refers to the expansion of a single business by extending its own operations, using retained profits and loan capital. It usually involves steady growth, planned over a long time period.
>
> **Inorganic growth** refers to expansion by merger or takeover of an existing business. It can be a quick way to grow – the business will increase in size immediately. But it can be risky.

Many businesses expand organically when they are relatively small. Organic growth is often less risky than **inorganic growth**. It suits businesses that have a single successful brand with growth potential. There may be fast-growing demand for its products or it may diversify into new markets or take market share from competing businesses.

M&A

Companies differ in their views as to whether it is better to develop their own product range or to acquire successful brands and technologies through takeovers and mergers. In Japan most businesses grow organically. In the UK and USA takeovers are quite frequent when the economy is growing; they are part of 'normal' business activity. Sometimes the easiest way to achieve larger scale production is to merge with another company. Alternatively, a takeover may be the best way forward – this is known as acquisition.

WATCH OUT!

Make sure you understand the work you have done recently on economies of scale (Chapter 5) and mergers and takeovers (Chapter 6).

Methods of growing organically

Economies of scale

On the most basic level, organic growth simply means investing in production facilities, taking on more employees and selling more output. In many cases this will lead to economies of scale. If costs are lower, prices can be cut to attract more customers. Alternatively prices can be kept the same, so that profits increase, helping to provide finance for further investment and expansion.

Apple

The overwhelming factor in Apple's growth has been its pursuit of organic growth. It has averaged only one acquisition per year for the past 25 years and most of these were comparatively small companies that had distinctive capabilities that Apple could use.

Apple's own distinctive capability is rooted in its culture of innovation and its intense focus on a relatively small range of products. (Think of Unilever, with its 400 different brands, many acquired through takeovers.) Apple is different – it produces a range of mobile phones, computers and tablets, but its focus is entirely on innovative electronic products with a very distinctive style.

Apple doesn't compete on price, although some customers would argue that it does offer value for money. It doesn't bother doing a great deal of market research – Steve Jobs thought that if you produce something that has outstanding qualities, people would decide that they needed it, regardless of whether they wanted it before they saw it in action. By early 2016, Apple had accumulated retained profits of US$102 billion.

Google and Microsoft have been very much more active than Apple in taking over other businesses.

Show your understanding

Explain the fundamental drivers of Apple's success.

Explain the importance of retained profits in Apple's strategy.

Competitive-ness

Small businesses grow organically if they have a competitive product. Restaurant chains may start with just one outlet that succeeds in attracting customers. If most of the tables get booked ahead, it makes sense to open another restaurant in a similar neighbourhood. Economies of scale are not really relevant; simply by duplicating a good idea, the business can expand. This type of growth may be possible in quite a wide range of service sector activities. Another way to grow is to set up franchises. Specific examples include Pizza Hut and Ovenclean but there are many other franchise operations, for example in the hotel business.

In manufacturing, a rather different pattern is common. Organic growth may require some combination of these factors:

● innovative R&D – employing people with specialist skills may be important.

● cutting costs by using new technologies to increase competitiveness.

● product diversification – new product development may open up more and bigger markets.

Marketing

● vigorous marketing strategies that introduce existing products to a wider market, sometimes involving new foreign markets.

These strategies can figure in inorganic growth too. But for businesses that aim to grow organically, some or all may be essential. Diversification is a key factor for Ikea, which is constantly enlarging both its product portfolio and its geographical locations. For Apple the key factor is innovation – enough on its own to bring success in many markets. The strategies highlighted in Ansoff's matrix may lead to many opportunities.

Notice the extent to which organic growth is based on competitiveness. This may involve price or non-price competition. Using new technologies can cut costs and also foster new product developments and quality improvements. But even without new technologies, some businesses thrive organically simply by designing attractive products or mounting a successful advertising campaign that attracts new customers.

> **Show your understanding**
> Identify one business that has not been mentioned in this chapter and has grown organically. Explain how it has achieved its current situation.

Corporate strategy

The strategic portfolio

Decisions concerning organic and inorganic growth are at the heart of corporate strategy. Planning for growth can involve a choice between the two alternatives but over time, many businesses grow in both ways. Usually however, there is emphasis on one or the other.

When a company reviews its strategic portfolio – its range of products – it is considering the areas of business in which its future lies. It looks at its existing portfolio, alongside its distinctive capabilities. (These figured in Chapter 2, along with SWOT analysis and Ansoff's matrix.) What are its strengths and how can these be harnessed to secure a competitive advantage in the future? Few markets stand still and allow the company to continue with business as usual. Markets are dynamic, constantly changing, and maintaining a competitive edge requires forward planning. Survival may require constant innovation in both products and production processes, to stay competitive with the best in the field.

Some businesses chose to merge with or take over competing businesses, using this strategy to diversify into completely different products and markets, becoming conglomerates. Others like to avoid the risks of inorganic growth and grow on their own; this may take longer but perhaps be more profitable in the long run. If the business succeeds it will at least maintain its market share and it may achieve significant growth in sales.

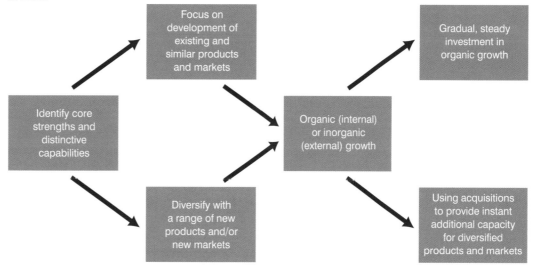

Advantages of organic growth

Corporate cultures

Organic growth is often less risky than inorganic growth. It is sometimes difficult to tell in advance of a merger or takeover what the likely difficulties might be. Possible risk factors include:

● Two merging companies may have very different corporate cultures – ways of working and attitudes and values that become embedded in individual businesses. It is difficult to merge differing cultures – it may take time and may possibly cause resentment amongst the staff of both businesses. (Corporate cultures were discussed in Chapter 6.) At best, there may still be misunderstandings. Growing organically, the business can retain all its cultural values and work in the same way as it has done in the past; growth creates much less disruption. (There is more detail on corporate culture in Chapter 14.)

Risks

- Sometimes the process of amalgamating two businesses turns out to be difficult simply because of differences in production processes. (See pages 31-2 for detail on the way things can go wrong, and the example of eBay and Skype.)

- It can be expensive to acquire a successful and profitable business. There may be unexpected costs that make profitability hard to achieve. The legal and contractual costs of a complex merger can be considerable. If the merger works to create a more efficient and profitable outcome this may not matter. But if other impediments emerge, success may be unattainable.

Apple's tradition of innovation has created an especially powerful body of product developers who are used to generating ideas on a continuous basis.

Organic growth exploits the qualities that the business has developed in the past and uses them to create a strategy for growth in the future. Think of Apple. Its tradition of innovation has created an especially powerful body of product developers who are used to generating ideas on a continuous basis. Ikea simply takes its business model to new markets by setting up both production facilities and sales outlets in new locations and different countries.

Joint ventures

Organic growth can involve expanding markets by setting up new branches in other countries. Distinctive capabilities can be replicated in markets further and further afield, sometimes operating as joint ventures to help the business adjust to the new location.

> **Example**
> JCB, the earth-moving and construction equipment company, set up as a family business in 1945 and created a subsidiary company in India in 1979. It now has several factories there as well as sales outlets and training schemes. It remains a private family business. They identify customer focus and quality as their crucial attributes.

Organic growth does not prevent businesses from developing in new ways. Retained profits can be used to invest in radically different approaches to production. Implementing new technologies or adopting new ways of organising the business can work well.

> **Think!**
> How has on-line retailing helped to create organic growth? Provide some examples.

Some business managers plan mergers and takeovers because they relish the prospect of enhanced status and power that they may achieve. In reality, they might be much better off staying with the organic approach, looking at the needs of the business rather than the potential excitement of a takeover and the publicity it will generate.

Against the organic approach

Inorganic growth

Organic growth can be a very slow process. Inorganic growth, via mergers and acquisitions (M&A) allows a business to expand quickly, using all the facilities of the business that has been merged with or taken over. Customers, sales, market share and assets of the acquired business are gained, often at a lower cost than if developed through organic growth.

Inorganic growth can bring many benefits:

- It can be a very quick way to diversify. It can add vitality to an existing but tired product range, or open up a new market where the other business already has a strong presence. This may be much quicker than developing new products and markets internally.

- It may provide an opportunity to achieve a higher level of brand recognition.

Efficiency

- Managers can benefit from the expertise of another business already operating in the market, making use of complementary strengths.

- Inorganic growth can lead to new economies of scale. Rationalising processes helps to avoid duplication of resources (e.g. expensive equipment or a design team) and cuts costs of production. This can reduce overhead costs and increase efficiency.

- After a merger, parts of both businesses that are not performing well can be sold, so that efforts are concentrated where there is the greatest expertise, enhancing focus.

Brands

It is easy to acquire coveted brands, technologies, patents and markets by buying a competitor, quickly diversifying the product range. (In 1988 when Nestlé took over Rowntree, Nestlé said that what they most wanted was the KitKat brand. KitKat was the world's second-best selling chocolate product. Only the Mars bar sold more.)

New markets

A business that wants to start up in a new and unfamiliar market may be well advised to buy an existing company. If they want to start selling in China, they will be required to set up a joint venture (i.e. a partnership with a locally based business). This is especially useful for a business that wants to gain entry to a market that has barriers to entry, such as high import duties. It also helps where there are language barriers or cultural, social and legal problems are likely.

Many businesses believe that rationalising their activities will lead to cost savings and increase the value added by the business. A merger holds out hope of economies of scale, complementary strengths and increasing market share leading to synergy. Together, they hope, both businesses will be more successful than either could be on their own. This can happen but quite often, mergers and takeovers actually lead to disappointment and may even lead to subsequent divestment. Organic growth may not always be the better option but inorganic growth creates improvements only in about half of the cases concerned.

ANSWERS

Page 55, Investment appraisal

	Project A	Project B
Payback period	2 years 1 month	1 year 6 months
ARR	28%	23%
DCF	£20,480	£64,605

Page 92, Profit margins

	2015	2013	2011
Gross profit margin	90.0%	86.3%	78.8%
Operating profit margin	-4.8%	7.5%	16.6%

Page 94, Liquidity ratios – Question 1

	2015	2013	2011
Current ratio	1.9	1.5	4.7
Acid test ratio	1.7	1.5	4.4

(Some 2011 data included for interest but does not figure in the questions.)

Page 96, Gearing and ROCE performance ratios

	2015	2013	2011
Gearing	18%	21%	8.7%
ROCE	-3.4%	4.7%	10.4%

(Some 2011 data included for interest but does not figure in the questions.)

Chapter 8

Reasons for staying small

Chadwick's Brewery, Kendal, Cumbria

Tim Chadwick is a part-time teacher and part-time brewer of real ales. When he graduated, he took on a job at a local pub that brewed its own beer and became fascinated by the whole process. When the opportunity arose to buy some second-hand brewing equipment, he jumped at the chance and began working from a small business unit in Kendal. Tim produces four different beers and sells them to local pubs in the Lake District and Yorkshire Dales.

These 'guest' beers are produced in individual barrels and Tim is the chief brewer, salesman, accountant and delivery driver. He could expand and produce cheaper beer that would sell in greater quantities but prefers to produce a high quality product. Chadwick's Brewery has a lot of competition; there are 42 breweries in Cumbria alone, producing a wide range of beers and ciders. In addition, there are other small brewers in neighbouring counties, the supermarkets stock a wide range of bottled products and then there are the huge multinational brewing companies, such as the world's biggest, Anheuser-Busch InBev, with a range of global brands including Budweiser and Stella Artois.

Discussion points

What problems is Tim likely to face in his business?

How can he compete and survive in such a competitive market?

Small business survival in competitive markets

Distinctive capabilities

After earlier chapters you could be forgiven for thinking that the only way to succeed in business is to become big. That way you get the success and reap all the benefits of size and scale; lower average costs, increased profitability and market power. Yet even the most cursory of glances shows that to be successful you don't have to be big. For every Walmart or Tesco there are many small corner shops, for every Costa's or Starbucks there are local cafes and so on. Clearly, small businesses not only survive, they flourish. In fact, many have very distinctive capabilities that give them a competitive edge.

The vast majority of businesses are classed as small. The EU has an official definition of business size: medium-sized businesses are those with fewer than 250 employees, small-sized fewer than 50, and micro-sized fewer than 10. Together these are called SMEs (Small and Medium sized Enterprises). In the EU and the UK over 99% of all businesses are classed as SMEs.

A UK government report from October 2015 produced the following statistics...

- At the start of 2015 there were 5.4 million private sector businesses.

Small businesses

- SMEs accounted for 99.3% of all private sector businesses.

- SMEs employed 15.6 million people or 60% of all private sector employment in the UK.

- The annual turnover of SMEs was £1.8 trillion, 47% of all private sector turnover in the UK.

Small businesses are a crucial part of our economy in terms of employment, output and wealth creation. In addition, they are often responsible for much of the creative innovation that provides us with progress and the products and services of the future. Don't forget, today's small firms could turn out to be the global giants of tomorrow. Think of Bill Gates, starting Microsoft or Steve Jobs and that first Apple computer.

> ### ⚠️ WATCH OUT!
>
> In Theme 1, Section 1.5.3, you learnt about the reasons for setting up a business. Profit and sales maximisation are important objectives that drive businesses forward. But you also learnt about survival and satisficing. Some entrepreneurs are simply not interested in growth because they are happy if they can make a living out of the business. They may enjoy being self-employed, maybe making hand-made products or designing and creating gardens, or working as electricians or carpenters. Staying small looks good to many.

Product differentiation and USPs

Distinctiveness and price

One obvious way to survive is to have something about your product or service that is different from anyone else's. When faced with a competitive market place, producers may try to make their product stand out from all the other similar, if not identical, products. Any difference perceived by the consumer gives an advantage, in terms of sales and profit. By being different a product is perhaps more likely to be bought than a rival which is undifferentiated. Not only that, but once seen as being different and hence more desirable, price can be increased. The greater the difference, the more that price can be increased.

> ### Examples
>
> Cream O' Galloway make and sell ice cream in SW Scotland but differentiate their product from the mass market by only using organic ingredients. Beyond Skin sell shoes but their shoes do not use any animal products such as leather and are aimed at vegans and vegetarians. Both businesses benefit from this differentiation and are able to build up a loyal customer base.

The key feature of a product that really differentiates it from the competition is its USP or Unique Selling Point. As the name implies a USP is unique and applicable to that business. This may be the product itself, or an aspect of the product, or the way it is marketed, in fact anything that makes potential customers notice that product and buy it. For Toblerone, the chocolate bar, the USP is its triangular shape; the Polo mint has a hole, Dr Marten's boots have that distinctive sole and Rice Krispies go 'Snap, Crackle and Pop'!

There are other organic ice cream manufacturers and other vegan shoemakers but within these differentiated areas there can be businesses that stand out even further. Charlie Francis set up his ice cream business, Lick me I'm delicious in 2011. His USP is that he makes ice cream using liquid nitrogen to freeze it giving it a silky smooth texture. His ice cream machines can be hired for parties and corporate functions along with his Edible Mist Orbs that create a flavoured inhalable micro mist. Toms Shoes also sells synthetic shoes but their USP is one for one. When Toms sells a pair of shoes, a new pair of shoes is given to an impoverished child.

> ### Think!
>
> Does Chadwick's Brewery have a USP?
>
> Are there any businesses close to you that you can identify as having a product differentiation strategy? Do any have a USP?

Flexibility in responding to customer needs

Responding to demand

In today's modern and competitive world consumers have come to expect instant service, with next day delivery and even same day delivery being offered by the likes of the big supermarkets and Amazon. While speed of service may be important for some customers, others are attracted by the flexibility that small businesses in particular can offer.

Big businesses have set procedures and ways of doing things; production systems tend to be specialised and geared towards one particular task and doing it well and efficiently. To change this can be difficult and time consuming. In general, small businesses have greater flexibility than larger ones and are better able to respond promptly to commercial or consumer demands. They are often capable of innovating and creating products and services more rapidly. This may be in response to rapidly changing social or economic trends. Small businesses can often respond to unusual or specific requests in a matter of days.

Flexibility

Small businesses know their customers well, much better than a large business does. If a modification is requested in the products or services offered or even the business's hours of operation, it is possible for a small business to make changes. Customers can even have a role in product development. Small businesses are often able to do this because their employees are more receptive to the values and needs of

Many small businesses cater for niche markets.

the business. By contrast, employees in larger businesses may be entrenched in a set pattern of working and less open to the flexibility needed.

There is a school of thought that during times of economic stability, large businesses do well because they can formulate long-term strategies that allow them to grow and expand, taking advantage of building strong identities and benefitting from economies of scale. However, during times of instability and economic uncertainty, such as the present era, the advantage may pass to the smaller businesses that have the flexibility to adapt and change.

Niche markets

Many small businesses cater for niche markets. They can survive by adapting to the preferences of their particular niche. Some may seek out additional niches, as a way of diversifying that will protect them from changes in tastes and fashions.

Customer service

'The customer is always right' is a well-known business saying but for many customers it is not the case. Even though many businesses have improved their customer service in recent years, there are still many people who have had poor experiences with large businesses; complaints of impersonal service, poor after-sales care and difficulties in getting complaints addressed are still numerous.

According to a CEI Survey, 86% of buyers will pay more for a better customer experience. Customer service has never been more important; satisfied customers not only remain loyal and come back for more but they will pass recommendations to their friends. This is much easier than trying to acquire new customers, which takes time, effort and money. In the current economic climate consumers are shopping around and demanding more value for money.

Competitive advantage

By focusing on customer service, small businesses can create a real competitive advantage. With their smaller size and closeness to their customers it should be easier to get customer service right. A small business can interact with the customer more closely and frequently; it can develop more of a personal relationship than a large business and this gives it an advantage. Larger businesses have many layers and often have systems that prevent closer contact with the customer. Complaints can be handled faster and on a more personal level in a small company, making long-term customer relations easier and more profitable.

e-commerce

The story of Amazon shows how e-commerce can spawn a huge business operation in a fairly short time. But many small businesses would not be alive now without the opportunities created by on-line advertising and ordering. Small businesses are often particularly suited to internet marketing because they can easily access and cater for specialised niche markets. They would have faced many more difficulties prior to the widespread use of the internet, which began in the mid-1990s. Before then, it would have needed costly advertising to reach potential niche customers.

Example

David Newbould is a painter who exhibits his work through Kingswear Gallery. The gallery is located on the outskirts of Leeds. Much of its business comes through its website. It exists to publicise artists' work, frame pictures and provide prints and digital images. It means that David's paintings are accessible world-wide. The gallery is located in a place that would not attract many visitors, but it can offer its services to anyone anywhere. As a business it is relatively small but it is a great deal more profitable than it could possibly be without the internet.

Niche advertising

Today, small businesses can be in direct contact with potential customers with very little outlay. The internet provides an efficient way of reaching customers on a global basis, giving them a platform to promote their goods and services and engage directly with customers. Technology has made it easier for a small business to communicate and grow. It is not just the commerce side of things but also the use of emails, social media, skype, plug-ins and apps that enable a small business to be more successful and competitive than it might have been in the past.

The internet has enabled a small business to gain an advantage in four main ways…

● **Customer base** – the internet gives a small business instant access to a global market.

● **24 hour access** – customers can access the business at any time and are no longer constrained by opening times or office hours.

● **Networking** – small businesses can find each other easily, interact and gain help, knowledge and useful contacts.

● **Costs** – the internet is very cost effective. It is far cheaper than maintaining a physical presence and it also allows business to be conducted without expensive travel.

Exam style question

The Cycle Jersey (TCJ) offer a custom design service that enables cyclists to design their own jerseys, either as a one-off, or for a group of friends going on a cycling trip or charity ride. TCJ offers a full service including design from your own ideas and production, all within two weeks and with the promise of 'excellent, personal customer service'.

Ella's Kitchen is a company that makes 100% organic baby and toddler food. It uses simple product names, such as 'the Purple One' blackcurrant juice, and 'Banana Baby Brekkie' rice meal, designed to appeal to children rather than adults. Its packaging is bright and colourful with lettering that mimics a child's writing, which helps the brand stand out from its less child-centric rivals on the shelf.

The Black Farmer produces a range of meat products including sausages and burgers. It uses only higher welfare RSPCA Assured British meat. It also supports the increasingly large community of people who have Coeliac disease, or a wheat and gluten intolerance; all products are gluten free. Founder Wilfred Emmanuel-Jones was born in Jamaica and brought up in inner-city Birmingham. His distinctive packaging and company name reflect his origins.

A Class Brides is a bridal boutique in Bristol which has won many awards including 'highly commended awards' from Wedding Ideas Magazine and the Bristol and Somerset Best Bridal Boutique in 2014 & 2015. They aim to offer a complete and individual service for brides and their families. They put their success down to customer recommendations and personal service.

1. Using the ideas in this chapter explain how each of these businesses has not only survived but become successful. *(8 marks)*

2. Explain why large businesses might find it hard to adopt the same strategies. *(6 marks)*

3. Assess the disadvantages of being a small business. *(10 marks)*

4. Assess possible strategies open to Tim to ensure the survival of Chadwick's brewery. *(12 marks)*

Chapter 9
Quantitative sales forecasting

Apple reports record second quarter results

In April 2015 Apple posted quarterly revenue of $58 billion, up from $45 billion in the same quarter the year before. Quarterly profits rose to $13.6 billion from $10.2 billion a year ago. This growth was fuelled by record sales of the iPhone, Mac and revenue from the App store. Tim Cook said "We're seeing a higher rate of people switching to iPhone than we've experienced in previous cycles, and we're off to an exciting start to the June quarter with the launch of the Apple Watch." At the same time sales of the iPad have not shown the same growth, and seem to be sharply seasonal.

Figure 9.1: Apple sales data (volume)

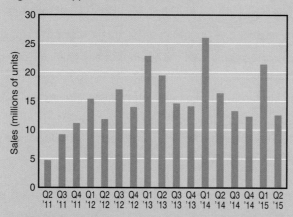

Questions
1. What conclusions might Apple draw from this data?
2. What other information would you need before deciding on a strategy?

Predictions

Many businesses will attempt to predict what is likely to happen to sales in the short to medium term and essentially, quantitative methods assume that what happened in the past is likely to some extent to happen again. There are two main methods of quantitative forecasting:

● A business may examine a relationship between two variables to see if one is affected by the other. For example, does increasing spending on advertising lead to a comparable increase in sales? This relationship is called a correlation.

● The second method uses past trends to make forecasts and this is called **time series analysis**.

Scatter graphs can be used to examine whether there is a relationship between two sets of variables; this would be a correlation. The business can then look at the strength of the correlation. If the data shows that there is a strong correlation between the amount spent on advertising and the level of sales, this could be used to justify further increases in the advertising budget. Similarly if there is a correlation between temperatures and sales, firms can use weather forecasts to influence production decisions.

Scatter graphs

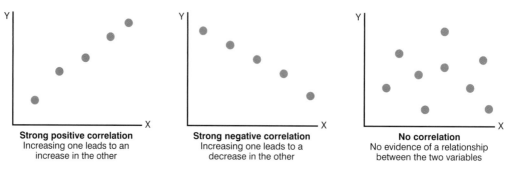

| **Strong positive correlation** | **Strong negative correlation** | **No correlation** |
| Increasing one leads to an increase in the other | Increasing one leads to a decrease in the other | No evidence of a relationship between the two variables |

> **Time series** provide short and long-term data which can be analysed over a period to provide information on likely future trends.
>
> **Scatter graphs** show the correlation between two sets of data over a period of time. If the points plotted on the graph seem to be randomly distributed there is no correlation and it is safe to conclude that there is no significant relationship between the two variables.

Calculation of time series analysis

When a business is attempting to forecast future sales or costs based on past data they will need to eliminate fluctuations in the data. This could be caused by unexpected events such as bad weather having an effect on sales, or expected events such as seasonality. By smoothing out the trends it is easier for firms to identify trends and therefore produce forecasts. This is done by calculating a **moving average**.

Three period moving average

The following data relates to sales figures for a business over a 16 year period. When forecasting, managers must examine whether the data shows an upward trend, or a period of stability. The figures based on raw data alone are not enough.

Table 9.1: Sales data, £m

2000	130
2001	120
2002	110
2003	115
2004	118
2005	132
2006	146
2007	138
2008	100
2009	95
2010	100
2011	105
2012	120
2013	125
2014	130
2015	140

Figure 9.2: Sales data, £m

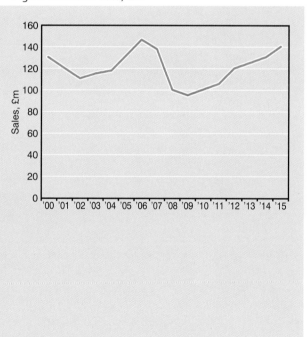

Cyclical variations

The data in Table 9.1 is plotted in Figure 9.2. There seems to be a **cyclical** pattern, but there is little sign of any trend on which a business can base a forecast. These **cyclical variations** can be a reflection of the business cycle. For example a luxury yacht maker or high end beauty business may experience a sharp drop in revenue during times of recession and a rise as the economy recovers, while the situation may be reversed for other businesses that do well during economic downturns (these are called **counter-cyclical**).

Calculating a **moving average** reveals any longer term trend by smoothing out peaks and troughs in the data. A three year moving average is calculated by adding years 1, 2 and 3 and dividing by 3 to get an average for the second year. The next average is calculated by eliminating year 1 and picking up year 4, therefore giving an average of years 2, 3 and 4. The results are shown in Table 9.2 below.

Table 9.2: The 3-year moving average

Year	Sales (£m)	3 Year Total	3 Year Moving Average	Variation
2000	130			
2001	120	360	120.00	0.00
2002	110	345	115.00	-5.00
2003	115	343	114.33	0.67
2004	118	365	121.67	-3.67
2005	132	396	132.00	0.00
2006	146	416	138.67	7.33
2007	138	384	128.00	10.00
2008	100	333	111.00	-11.00
2009	95	295	98.33	-3.33
2010	100	300	100.00	0.00
2011	105	325	108.33	-3.33
2012	120	350	116.67	3.33
2013	125	375	125.00	0.00
2014	130	395	131.67	-1.67
2015	140			

Line of best fit

By calculating a three year moving average the firm has smoothed out the fluctuations in the data as shown below, which makes it easier to plot a **line of best fit** and begin the process of forecasting sales. Using our data this shows that despite the cyclical variation the general trend shows sales are stable.

Figure 9.3: The 3-year moving average

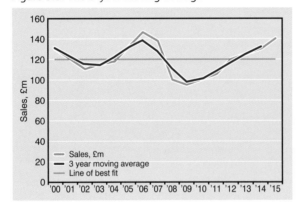

Variations

In an attempt to make forecasting more accurate, a firm will look at the **variation** (the difference between the average and the actual figure) as shown in the final column of Table 9.2. By adding these variations and dividing by the total number of variations a firm can calculate the **average variation**. In the example the average variation would be -0.48 (i.e. £-0.48 million). Reducing any point on the line of best fit by this amount should make the forecast more accurate.

Show your understanding
Explain how moving averages might help Apple to interpret the sales data in Figure 9.1.

Four quarter moving average with seasonal variation

Many firms will have products that sell better at different times of the year because of holidays, seasons or other factors. For example in the UK new number plates are released in March and September, and sales of new cars tend to increase during these periods. For this reason a four quarter moving average may be more appropriate. The principle of the moving average is the same, but the process is a little more complicated as there is no 'centre period' to put the average against.

Centring

The solution is to use a technique called **centring**, basically involving two steps:

1. Calculate the **four** and **eight** period moving totals to find a mid-point

2. Find the average by dividing the totals by eight.

We can use the following data for new car sales at a showroom to calculate a four quarter moving average. (Remember a quarter refers to a period of three months.)

Table 9.3: Quarterly new car sales £000

Seasonal changes

Year and Quarter	Sales (£000)	4 Quarter Total (£000)	8 Period Total (£000)	4 Quarter Moving Average (£000)	Variation
2012 Q1	240				
2012 Q2	280				
		1160			
2012 Q3	380		2340	292.5	87.5
		1180			
2012 Q4	260		2400	300	-40
		1220			
2013 Q1	260		2500	312.5	-52.5
		1280			
2013 Q2	320		2620	327.5	-7.5
		1340			
2013 Q3	440		2680	335	105
		1340			
2013 Q4	320		2700	337.5	-17.5
		1360			
2014 Q1	260		2760	345	-85
		1400			
2014 Q2	340		2820	352.5	-12.5
		1420			
2014 Q3	480		2900	362.5	117.5
		1480			
2014 Q4	340		3000	375	-35
		1520			
2015 Q1	320		3060	382.5	-62.5
		1540			
2015 Q2	380		3100	387.5	-7.5
		1560			
2015 Q3	500				
2015 Q4	360				

Interpretation of scatter graphs and line of best fit

Extrapolation

Whether a firm uses three period or four quarter moving averages, the intention is to smooth out any fluctuations in data and therefore be able to identify trends and produce forecasts.

Using the car sales data in Table 9.3 produces the graph in Figure 9.4. By adding a '**line of best fit**' through the data, the company is able to identify the trend and forecast future sales. This is called **extrapolation**.

Figure 9.4: Using a line of best fit

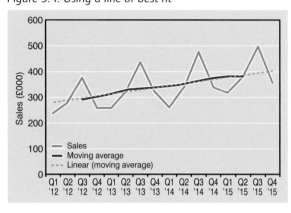

However using a line of best fit in this case will not produce accurate forecasts. It is clear from the graph and the data that sales fluctuate throughout the year with quarter 3 being above trend and quarter 1 being below. Therefore using a line of best fit for Q3 sales would underestimate their value and vice versa for Q1. To produce a more accurate forecast it is necessary to calculate a variation. Using our car sales example we can calculate the **seasonal variation**. This is done by looking at the actual figure for a quarter compared to the moving average. The results are shown in the final column in Table 9.3.

Seasonal variation

The business will then look at the average variation for each quarter. For example in Q1 the variations are -52.5, -85 and -62.5. Therefore the average variation for Q1 sales is (-52.5 + -85 + -62.5) ÷ 3 = – 66.67.

The firm can use these quarterly variations, together with their line of best fit, to produce more accurate forecasts. Using this method the quarterly variations are:

Q1 = -66.67
Q2 =   -9.17
Q3 = 103.33
Q4 = -30.83

> A **line of best fit** can be drawn on a scatter graph where there is a clear connection between two datasets. It will go through the middle of the points plotted on the graph. The closer the points are to the line of best fit, the closer the correlation will be. Statisticians have complex ways of calculating a line of best fit precisely but you may just draw a freehand line of best fit.
>
> **Extrapolation** means using the existing numerical data to estimate likely future values. Sales data expressed as a moving average can be extended to extrapolate expected future sales trends.
>
> **Variations** show fluctuations when sales are above or below the long term trend. *Average* variation refers to the overall difference from the trend. *Cyclical* variation occurs when there is an identifiable pattern over a longer period of time. *Seasonal* variation occurs when there is a regular pattern over a shorter identifiable period of time.

Limitations of quantitative sales forecasting techniques

Used in conjunction with other decision making techniques, time series analysis can be a useful forecasting tool. For example if a company has identified seasonal variations, it can take action at the most appropriate time. Furthermore, if the firm is in a relatively stable environment then forecasts will tend to be reasonably accurate, especially in the short term. However, on its own the technique has several flaws. It rests on the assumption that the past is a reliable indication of the future, which in a fast moving business environment may no longer hold true. The longer a firm attempts to forecast into the future, the less accurate the forecasts become and therefore there is a greater element of risk involved. As the name suggests, time series analysis only includes **quantitative** information which is based on facts and figures. A business will need to combine this with **qualitative** information to provide the narrative behind the data.

Qualitative information

You will have seen from Chapter 2 and 3 that there are also other factors, both internal and external, that will reduce the effectiveness of sales forecasting. Internally, the data used is only as good as its source. New smaller businesses will not have the same amount of past data as larger more established firms, so projections would be more difficult. In addition there are no guarantees that managers will act on the data, particularly if it contradicts their viewpoint. A manager with a track record of success, based on experience and 'hunch' decisions, may be more reluctant to wait until forecasts are calculated and strategies are formulated. This is especially true if the market is moving quickly and the business wants to gain **first mover advantage**.

First mover advantage

Externally there is a range of factors relating to PESTLE analysis (pages 15-17). These will, to varying degrees, affect the accuracy of any forecasts. For example how stable is the economic environment and is that the same in each country where the business operates? Has there been any change in the demographic profile? Is the speed of technological innovation changing the market? Are new laws planned which could affect costs or revenue? This is where qualitative information is needed. Each business will be affected differently by these changes and will need to examine their importance when forecasting.

Quantitative information provides data in numerical terms, based on figures collected over a period of time.

Qualitative information can be generated from past experience. It will usually be less precise than the numerical data but it may allow quantitative information to be analysed in a more nuanced way.

First mover advantage can be achieved by getting a product onto the market ahead of competing businesses.

Example

Netflix and the DVD market

In 2005 JVC ceased production of video recorders. For thirty years the VHS format had revolutionised viewing habits worldwide but as the new millennium started it was obvious there was a new kid on the block. DVDs had more functionality through the use of menus, did not need rewinding after use and the picture quality was far superior. Even the much lauded laser disk did not stand a chance as the market shifted. DVDs, then DVD recorders, then Blu Ray all followed in quick succession but even now it looks like discs will not dominate the market for as long as tapes did as consumers move towards downloadable media. Ken Ross, spokesman for Netflix said "We have known from the beginnings of Netflix more than a decade ago that DVDs would eventually become obsolete and content would be delivered to our members over the internet. The question for us has been how much to invest in streaming technology and content – and how quickly."

Questions

Time series forecasting

1. A major housebuilder, FZR Construction is considering purchasing land for a new residential development in Norwich. Their sales figures over the last ten years have fluctuated considerably and the company is looking at past data to try and identify any trends before they can devise a strategy. Sales for the last ten years are:

Year	2006	2007	2008	2009	2010	2011	2012	2013	2014	2015
Sales (£m)	8	12	10	16	18	10	8	6	14	16

(a) Calculate the **average** yearly sales for the company.

(b) Plot the sales figures on a graph.

(c) Company director Farah thinks the company should start producing homes at the higher priced end of the market. To what extent does the data support her decision?

2. Jacob and Isabelle run an independent sporting goods shop. Floor space is limited so they need to think carefully about their product range and the amount of stock they should keep. Their quarterly sales figures show some evidence of seasonality and the pair are considering the future. Jacob thinks that by targeting runners they can specialise in a niche part of the market. Isabelle thinks they need to widen their customer base by offering products that are more seasonal (e.g. snowboards and ski equipment in the winter, camping equipment and tennis clothing in the summer). They have produced the following quarterly sales figures from their accounts:

Year	Quarter	Sales £
2012	Q1	3,300
	Q2	2,200
	Q3	3,600
	Q4	3,400
2013	Q1	3,400
	Q2	4,300
	Q3	3,900
	Q4	4,100
2014	Q1	3,600
	Q2	4,500
	Q3	5,600
	Q4	6,400

(a) Plot the quarterly figures on a graph.

(b) Use the data to calculate a four quarter moving average.

(c) Add a line of best fit and suggest any future trend.

(d) Based on your analysis, which strategy should the company follow?

(Some answers on page 98)

Chapter 10

Investment appraisal

Kristiana Cosmetics

Kristiana Cosmetics makes a range of products that includes a specialist toothpaste. As part of a five-year plan to expand from niche health-food stores into high street outlets, the board of directors is considering investing £250,000 in a new production line. This will increase production volumes and speed. The production line is forecast to last for five years.

Discussion points
What questions would you encourage the board to ask before making this decision?

For each question you have identified, explain why this is important in the situation described above.

Investment decisions

All business operations incur costs. Some of these costs, called **revenue expenditure**, are for the purchase of goods or services which will be used up in the short term (usually within a year, in line with accounting practice). For example, raw materials may be stored for a short while but will then be used in the production process. Advertising payments generate a benefit (the advertising campaign) which is relatively short-lived.

Other costs are incurred by investment spending, i.e. **capital expenditure**. This refers to the purchase of fixed assets which are not immediately used up in production. Examples include premises, vehicles and machinery. They should continue to contribute to the success of a business over time and often they involve a significant cost. Because capital spending can involve large sums of money, managers need to be confident that their investment is worthwhile. After all, most businesses exist to make profit; money must be spent wisely.

So, how does a business decide:

Financial and opportunity costs

● whether a new capital investment is worth the financial and opportunity cost that it will incur? For example, whether or not to build a new distribution centre for a supermarket chain.

● between competing investment options, such as three possible sites for this new distribution centre?

Investment appraisal refers to techniques used to support decision making. Three methods of judging potential investments are introduced in this chapter. For each method, make sure that you know how to calculate it, how to interpret the figures that you produce and the limitations of the technique in helping to evaluate investments.

Methods of Investment Appraisal

Simple Payback	Average (Accounting) Rate of Return	Net Present Value

Revenue expenditure is spending on things that will be used only once in a business, for example current assets (stocks) and expenses such as utility bills or office stationery.

Capital expenditure is money spent on fixed assets such as machinery, vehicles and buildings. These remain in the business for a long period of time and can be used repeatedly.

Investment appraisal involves using techniques to decide whether to proceed with capital expenditure.

Estimating expected cash flows

Before starting an investment appraisal, the business must calculate the expected cash flows generated over the life of the investment. In the case study above, the toothpaste production line equipment is forecast to last for five years. During this time it will incur maintenance costs of £10,000 per year, in addition to the cost of the investment (outflows), and will contribute additional income of £100,000 per year (inflows). The forecast of expected cash flows will be based on available information, which might include:

● data on all input costs.

● past experience within the business, if this exists.

● independent test results, such as those conducted by trade bodies.

● the 'best guess' of managers, based on market research data and industry knowledge.

Cash flows

It is conventional to show the initial investment being made in year 0 (the present day). Each following year then shows the spending and revenue earned over that year. The cash flow estimate for the toothpaste production line might look something like this:

Year	Cash in (£)	Cash out (£)	Net cash flow (£)	Cumulative cash flow (£)
0	–	(250,000)	(250,000)	(250,000)
1	110,000	(10,000)	100,000	(150,000)
2	110,000	(10,000)	100,000	(50,000)
3	110,000	(10,000)	100,000	50,000
4	110,000	(10,000)	100,000	150,000
5	110,000	(10,000)	100,000	250,000
Total	**550,000**	**(300,000)**	**250,000**	**250,000**

Estimates

Each technique of investment appraisal uses this cash flow estimate to explore aspects of the investment decision. So it is important that cash flow estimates are not over-optimistic. Obviously they are estimates and reality may turn out to be different, particularly where predictions are based on limited information or in volatile market conditions.

Simple payback

This is a measure of how long it takes for the net cash flow generated by an investment to repay the initial outlay. The result is expressed as time: in years or years and months.

$$\text{Payback} = \frac{\text{cost of initial investment}}{\text{net cash earned per time period}}$$

Example

For Kristiana Cosmetics, the calculation would be £250,000 ÷ £100,000 because the investment is forecast to earn £100,000 per year. This gives a payback duration of 2.5 years, or 2 years and 6 months.

Tip: If payback is achieved in the middle of a year, calculate the monthly net cash flow for the final year and use this to determine the month when payback occurs.

Repayment

> **Simple payback** calculates the length of time needed for income generated by an investment to repay the cost of that investment.

Interpreting

The shorter the payback period, the better: it reduces the risk of the investment failing and the money being lost. The money is returned to the business more quickly and can therefore be reinvested in another project. Businesses with weak cash flow, in particular, may only be willing to invest in projects which will yield a quick payback.

Covering costs

If the payback period falls between two years, consider whether income is likely to be evenly spread throughout the year. For Kristiana Cosmetics this is likely to be the case as toothpaste demand fluctuates little. But for a business making Christmas decorations, the majority of sales will be at the end of the year, so the payback figure may not be reached until rather later.

If the payback period is close to the expected life span of the investment, there will be little leeway if cash inflows are lower than expected. If the total cash flow generated fails to cover the cost of the investment the business will make a loss on this project.

Limitations

Calculating the payback period is simple and therefore attractive. However, it doesn't consider what happens after the payback point is reached or how much profit is eventually likely. Remember, at the point of payback the investment has not been profitable – it has just covered its costs. Payback doesn't take into account the total profit generated over the life of the investment and could therefore rule out investments which would, over a longer period of time, be successful. For this reason it is common to use payback as a way to screen out projects with unacceptably long payback periods and then to compare remaining options using additional tools of analysis.

Profitability

Advantages of payback	Limitations of payback
• It is simple to calculate.	• It doesn't measure profitability.
• It is easy to understand.	• It doesn't acknowledge what happens after the payback period.
• It takes account of the timings of cash flows.	• It can encourage a focus on the short term rather than a more strategic approach.

Average rate of return

Return on investment

All business decisions carry an opportunity cost. Resources invested in a given project cannot then be invested elsewhere, so the lost benefit of this alternative investment is the 'cost' of committing to the first investment. Average Rate of Return (ARR) is a way of calculating the annual return on investment generated by a project. This enables easy comparison between rival projects even if their initial costs are different, and helps to identify which gives the best percentage return on investment. It also means that the returns from an investment can be compared with the likely interest that would be earned if the money were simply put in the bank. (At the time of writing current interest rates are very low compared to the past but this could change.)

$$\text{ARR} = \frac{\text{average profit}}{\text{cost of initial investment}} \times 100$$

To calculate the average profit, simply divide the net profit (or net total cash flow) figure from the cash flow prediction by the life of the investment in years. The answer to the ARR calculation is expressed as a percentage return per year of the initial investment.

Example

For Kristiana Cosmetics the calculation would be $\frac{(£250,000 \div 5)}{£250,000} \times 100$ or $\frac{£50,000 \times 100}{£250,000} = 20\%$ per year

In this case, investing in the production line machinery is forecast to generate an average profit per year of 20% of the initial investment.

The **average rate of return** of an investment shows the average annual profit generated by the investment over its lifetime as a percentage of the cost of investment.

Interpreting

The higher the ARR, the better, because this shows that money invested is being increased at a greater rate per year, on average. The directors might regard 20% as a good rate of return, though their final decision would probably depend on comparisons with the figures for alternative investments.

Limitations

Consider these two projects:

Comparing projects

		Project ABC (£)	Project XYZ (£)
Investment	*Year 0*	(10,000)	(10,000)
Cash inflows	*Year 1*	6,000	2,000
	Year 2	5,000	5,000
	Year 3	2,000	6,000
Total cash inflows		13,000	13,000
Total net profit		3,000	3,000
Average annual profit		3000 ÷ 3 = 1,000	3000 ÷ 3 = 1,000
Average rate of return		1,000 ÷ 10,000 x 100 = 10% per year	1,000 ÷ 10,000 x 100 = 10% per year

The ARR of each project is the same, but project ABC looks preferable. The payback period for ABC is less than two years, whereas for XYZ payback is not reached until halfway through year 3. It is beneficial to earn back the investment promptly so that this cash can be reinvested elsewhere.

When considering ARR, remember that it takes no account of the timing of cash inflows from a project. For this reason it may be best to consider this method of investment appraisal alongside another, such as the payback period or, as you will see below, the net present value.

Think!
Discuss with a partner the type of projects which might give the returns outlined in the table above. Identify strategies for improving the ARR or the payback period in each case.

Advantages of ARR	Limitations of ARR
• It includes all cash flows over the life of the project. • It is easy to compare with alternative investments of different amounts.	• It takes no account of the timing of cash flows.

Discounted cash flow (net present value)

DCF

Looking at the forecast cash flows for Kristiana Cosmetics, it seems that the earnings will be the same in each year. In reality, whilst earnings in each year are forecast to be the same, they are worth less to a business in the future than they are now. The business would prefer to have the money now, rather than in the future. Having the money now means it could be invested and start earning interest or dividends right away.

Money now

If the interest rate now is 10%, having the full £500,000 of forecast net cash inflows in the bank from day 1 would increase the amount available to spend in years 1-5 because it could be put in the bank to earn interest. By not having it available from the outset, the worth 'now' of the forecast income in the future falls by the amount of the current interest rate each year, because this is interest which the money could have earned if it had not been invested. For each additional year that a payment is delayed, it loses more value because it could have earned more interest.

NPV

The net present value (NPV), therefore, is the equivalent amount in today's money that future forecast earnings will be worth. The NPV is always lower than the estimated income shown in the initial cash flow estimate.

To take account of this loss of value we multiply future earnings by a discount factor. This reduces the earnings figure based on the time span and prevailing interest rate. You will be given discount factors should you need to use them; you do not need to calculate them. Discount factors for three different interest rates are shown here:

Future years	5% interest: discount rate	10% interest: discount rate	15% interest: discount rate
1	0.952	0.909	0.870
2	0.906	0.826	0.756
3	0.863	0.751	0.658
4	0.822	0.683	0.572
5	0.784	0.621	0.497

To allow for the loss of interest earned on money received in the future, we multiply the future amount by the corresponding discount factor. This reduces the future value to give the equivalent amount 'now'.

Money later

Example

The discounting calculations for Kristiana Cosmetics, assuming a constant interest rate of 10%, would look like this:

Year 1 (£100,000 received in 1 year's time): £100,000 x 0.909 = £90,900 current value
Year 2 (£100,000 received in 2 years' time): £100,000 x 0.826 = £82,600 current value
Year 3 (£100,000 received in 3 years' time): £100,000 x 0.751 = £75,100 current value
Year 4 (£100,000 received in 4 years' time): £100,000 x 0.683 = £68,300 current value
Year 5 (£100,000 received in 5 years' time): £100,000 x 0.621 = £62,100 current value

Total: £379,000 current value

This tells us that the forecast earnings of £500,000 over 5 years are worth £379,000 today at an interest rate of 10%. This is because investing £379,000 now at 10% would yield the same amount over 5 years, including interest payments.

Of course, we have to take account of the initial cash outflow of £250,000. There is no discount factor applied to this as it happens now – in year 0 when money has not yet 'lost' any value. We can summarise the NPV calculations in a table:

Discount factors

Year	10% discount factor	Net cashflow	DCF
0	–	(£250,000)	(£250,000)
1	0.952	£100,000	£90,900
2	0.826	£100,000	£82,600
3	0.751	£100,000	£75,100
4	0.683	£100,000	£68,300
5	0.621	£100,000	£62,100
NPV			£129,000

Therefore the net profit, after 5 years, from the new production line machinery, after repaying the initial investment, would be £379,000-£250,000 = £129,000, in today's money. This is significantly less than the £250,000 profit forecast in the initial cash flow estimate. However, it still represents a very healthy return on an investment of £250,000. Because the NPV is greater than 0, it shows us that investing in this project is forecast to earn more income for Kristiana Cosmetics than simply investing the £250,000 initial capital in the bank at 10%. Based on these figures, therefore, the project looks financially attractive.

> **Discounted cash flow** (**DCF**) is the process of adjusting future earnings to allow for the loss of value of money over time. One method of calculating DCF is **net present value**.
>
> The **net present value** (**NPV**) of an investment calculates the lifetime profit generated by the investment, with future earnings discounted to allow for the opportunity cost of the capital invested.

Interpreting

An NPV greater than zero should be the minimum expected value for a project. The higher the NPV, the better. You can see that the discount factors get more punitive as the interest rate rises or the length of time increases. This is to reflect the greater 'loss' incurred in these conditions, by not having the money now. One benefit of this method is that it is relatively easy to model the effect of different interest rates – calculations can be repeated using different discount factors to reflect a range of possible market situations, from cautious to wildly optimistic.

It is possible that forecast future earnings, when discounted, are less than the cost of the initial investment. In this case the project would have a negative NPV and would be effectively losing money. It would be wise not to invest in such a project as the money would earn more if invested elsewhere.

Limitations

As you have learned, the interest rate set by the Bank of England affects rates offered by banks, and this can change from month to month. This means that any assumptions made about interest rates in the future will only be guesses, as will the discount rate applied in calculations.

Calculating NPV is a complex process. It is also tricky to explain to others, so some stakeholders may not fully understand the calculations. It is important that calculations are accurate and understood if they are used to make big business decisions.

Unlike ARR, NPV figures cannot easily be compared for projects where the initial investment is not the same.

Advantages of DCF	Limitations of DCF
• It can model a proposed investment using different discount factors to reflect a range of market conditions. • Timing of cash flows and the opportunity cost of money are considered within the calculation.	• Detailed calculations are needed. • It is not easy to compare projects with differing initial investment amounts. • There is no consideration of the payback period.

Choosing which method of investment appraisal to use

The choice of method(s) will depend on the nature of the project and the resources available to the business. Time, money and skill are needed to collect the data required to make realistic, reliable forecasts. This is often difficult for small businesses so decisions about investments may be based on 'hunches' rather than detailed analysis. At the top end of the business world, job roles are created to research, model and report before decisions are reached.

Investment decisions are influenced by currently low inflation and interest rates. If inflation rates are rising there will be increased uncertainty. Lower interest rates make borrowing cheaper and will affect the outcome of discounted cash flow calculations. Some businesses need also to consider the international trading environment.

Interest rates vary

Market conditions

Benefits of investment appraisal

What if? scenarios

● It enables managers to compare options using (fairly) objective measures. These can be modelled to explore 'what-if?' scenarios. So decisions should be more robust, profits increased and the risk of failure reduced.

● It forces managers to examine planned capital expenditure carefully, which should increase understanding and therefore reduce the risk of making poor investment decisions.

● Evidence of investment appraisal can act as justification for spending decisions to shareholders and other stakeholders. This may be important, e.g. when a project makes a loss and shareholders want to apportion blame for this.

Limitations of investment appraisal

● The difficulty of making accurate forecasts could reduce the accuracy of assumptions that underpin calculations. This could be due to limited existing knowledge of likely costs and revenues or changing market conditions that distort forecasts over time.

Assumptions

● Much of the data underpinning investment appraisal rests on forecasts, so there is potential for managers to manipulate data so as to promote a personal viewpoint. It is important to be clear about the justification for forecasts and assumptions made.

● Focusing only on the financial aspect of a decision may miss out key qualitative issues. Generally, the best decisions consider qualitative as well as quantitative data. For example, the pros and cons of potential investments should be considered within the context of corporate objectives, strengths and market position as well as finances. A project with high short-term returns which causes environmental or social damage may lead to a costly loss of reputation and brand value.

Qualitative issues

● The time and money cost of conducting a detailed investment appraisal may not be possible for small businesses or for those needing to make a quick decision – e.g. when replacing vital equipment which has broken and is needed urgently.

Show your understanding

A business has two possible investment projects – Project A and Project B. Data for each project are summarised below:

		Project A (£)	Project B (£)
Capital outlay	(Year 0)	(25,000)	(90,000)
Return	Year 1	12,000	75,000
	Year 2	12,000	30,000
	Year 3	12,000	30,000
	Year 4	12,000	30,000
	Year 5	12,000	30,000

The current interest rate is 10%. Discount rates are given below:

Year	Discount rate
1	0.909
2	0.826
3	0.751
4	0.683
5	0.621

(a) For each project calculate:
- Payback
- ARR
- Net present value   *(Answers on page 37)*

(b) Based on your calculations, evaluate which project the business should select.

(c) Identify and explain three other factors, aside from the data you have calculated, which could influence the final choice of project undertaken.

Chapter 11

Decision trees

At last!

A pharmaceutical company has carried out some research and believes it has found a revolutionary new pimple cream. The cream is at an early stage of development and the head of Research and Development now has to decide how to proceed.

Focus group market research suggests that, if successfully brought to market, the cream could generate revenue of £22m. Further development costs would total £2m. At any stage in development the cream could be withdrawn from manufacture if it is found to be unsafe, and the money invested would be lost. Alternatively, the company could sell the cream now, at its current stage of development, to a rival skincare company, for them to bring to market. This would generate £5m in guaranteed income.

Discussion points

You have been asked to advise on how the company should proceed. What would you propose?

What criteria will influence your choice of strategy?

What additional information would help you to make a decision?

Business leaders make decisions all the time. Some, such as how much stock to order this week, are routine and simple. Others, such as the choice of caterer for a lunchtime business meeting, have a limited financial and strategic impact and do not require detailed analysis. This chapter is concerned with larger decisions that are significant in terms of cost, potential revenue and perhaps their impact on the future of the organisation.

Dealing with uncertainty

With important decisions to make, as in the case study above, business leaders want to ensure that they are making the 'best' decision. In itself, 'best' is a difficult concept: different appraisal tools (ARR, payback, NPV), each value a different aspect of the investment. Each tool assumes that certain outcomes will occur. If we want to allow for the uncertainty that is inherent in all decision making, we may choose a different tool to explore each potential outcome of a decision. One of these is the decision tree.

What is a decision tree?

In the case study above, you would recognise that your goal was to maximise the income generated by the cream. You probably saw the difficulty in allowing for uncertainty about whether or not further development would be successful. You weighed the potential 'best case' scenario of £20m possible profit against a guaranteed income of £5m or even a £2m loss.

A decision tree is a diagram which accounts for the uncertainty associated with business decisions. It structures a logical approach to decision making by attaching quantitative values to all possible outcomes. It includes a consideration of how likely it is that each possible outcome will actually happen. This leads to the identification of a single 'best' decision which should be taken. A decision tree may be used when there is some uncertainty but the likelihood of an outcome can be estimated.

Probability

> A **decision tree** is a diagram which shows all possible outcomes of a decision, together with the estimated probability and the expected monetary value of each of these outcomes.

Both risk and uncertainty are unavoidable. Risk can be quantified but uncertainty is about unknowns. However, in constructing a decision tree, we estimate the probabilities of uncertain events. Normally, probabilities are based on data collected over time. With decision trees, we will sometimes be estimating probabilities that cannot be based on past data.

Constructing a decision tree

1. A decision tree is constructed from left to right. Decisions and events are laid out in the order in which they occur.

Decision points

2. Each point at which a decision has to be taken is represented by a square (the decision point). Decisions are under the control of the business. The possible decisions are shown as lines leading from this square. The cost of each decision is shown under the line as a negative number.

Chance nodes

3. After each decision there are possible outcomes, or chance events. This is shown by a circle (a chance node). The possible outcomes from each decision are shown as lines leading from this circle. Outcomes are not under the control of the business.

4. The monetary gain (or loss) from each outcome is shown at the far right of the diagram.

Figure 11.1

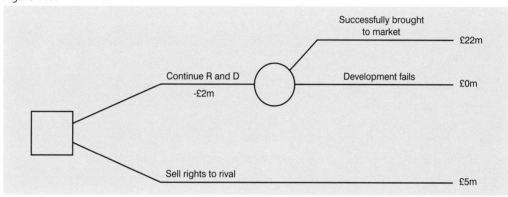

Figure 11.1 lays out all the possible decisions and outcomes for this event. Looking at the diagram, it seems obvious that the firm should continue R&D and then successfully bring the cream to market, because this is the outcome with the greatest financial reward. The problem is that the cream may not sell well. It is a chance outcome whether the cream succeeds or fails. More information is needed.

5. For each possible outcome, the chance, i.e. probability, of this occurring is estimated. This is shown below the line representing this outcome, usually as a decimal. Some outcomes are more likely than others – these will have a higher probability. To calculate the probability linked to each event, a business may use information such as market research data or previous sales figures, to come up with a 'best guess' of the likelihood of each outcome. The total of all probabilities leading from a chance node must equal 1, because it is 'certain' that one of the outcomes will occur. (In mathematics, 1 represents certainty when calculating probability.)

Calculating probability

Figure 11.2

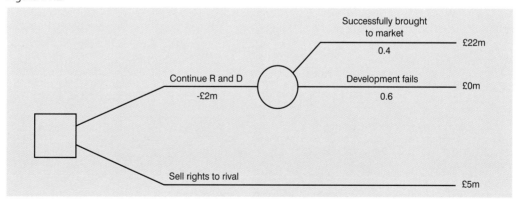

Note that there is no probability for the option 'sell rights to rival'. This is because there is only one possible outcome from this, so the probability of its happening is 1. It is certain.

In this example, the business has calculated that failure during development is more likely than success. They think there is a 40% chance of getting the cream to market and a 60% chance of failure. This has been shown on the diagram using the decimals 0.4 and 0.6. Note – these two figures add up to 1 because it is 'certain' that one or the other will occur.

On decision trees, greater uncertainty is represented by a lower probability figure – this means that the outcome is less likely to occur. The higher the figure, the more likely it is that the outcome will happen.

Probability of failure

6. Because it is not certain that continuing with R&D will lead to a successful launch, it isn't logical to assume that choosing to continue will *definitely* lead to earnings of £22m. Using the probability figures and the income figures together, we can allow for this uncertainty in the decision tree.

The probability figures tell us what would be likely to happen if the decision was taken many times. In this case, in 4 times out of 10, the launch would succeed (£22m income), and 6 times out of ten it would fail (£0 income). We can therefore calculate the *weighted average* income by multiplying the probability by the outcome in the following way:

Weighted average

$$
\begin{array}{llll}
& 0.4 \times £22\text{m} & & £8.8\text{m} \\
+ & 0.6 \times £0 & \text{or} \quad + & £0 \\
\hline
= & £8.8\text{m} & = & £8.8\text{m}
\end{array}
$$

Note – this figure is not what the company will really gain from deciding to continue with R&D. Rather, it is shorthand for saying '£22m, with a 40% chance of getting this amount'.

Expected value

Based on this calculation, we can see that the average or expected value of the decision to continue with R&D is £8.8m. We add this figure to the decision tree at the chance node arising from the decision.

Figure 11.3

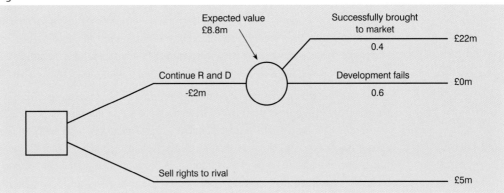

7. The decision is based on the financial benefit of each decision – the **expected value**. In the diagram above, choosing to continue R&D will net, on average, a profit of £6.8m (£8.8m – £2m development costs). Selling the cream's production rights to a rival will net only £5m, which is less than the alternative. Based on this, the company would choose to continue R&D. The decision(s) not taken are shown on a decision tree by striking through the decision line:

Figure 11.4

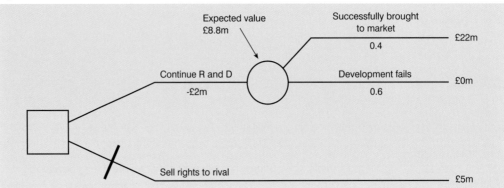

Decisions to be made occur where the business has choices. In the diagram these are represented by a square node (decision point). Businesses have control over decisions.

Chance events are possible outcomes resulting from a decision. In a decision tree diagram these are represented by a circular chance node. Businesses do not have direct control over possible outcomes – they are determined by chance.

Expected value – the monetary value of a decision, calculated by totaling the weighted average of each possible outcome of that decision.

Interpreting a decision tree

A simple decision tree is easy to interpret. As the branches of the tree get longer, and with more possible outcomes and decisions, a logical approach is required.

Calculating expected values

Calculations can be summarised in a table. Start on the right side of your diagram and work from right to left. Label each final outcome with a monetary value and probability. Then transfer all necessary information to the first columns of the table. This gives you the data needed to complete expected value calculations for each chance node. Now annotate your diagram with expected values at each node and cross out all branches except that with the highest value. Repeat for each intermediate stage of decisions or outcomes which remain.

Florence has a chain of retail stores in the UK. She wants to expand her business and is considering entering the German market. Moving quickly would give her the opportunity to gain market share before competitors open up, but taking the time to conduct detailed market research would improve her chances of success. Alternatively, Florence could stay in the UK and build her business in the existing market. After conducting initial research, Florence has identified four possible strategies:

A. Carry out detailed market research before expanding into Germany (cost £250,000).

B. Launch rapidly in the German market (cost £230,000).

C. Open a new store in the UK (cost £90,000).

D. Increase advertising of existing UK stores (cost £20,000).

Florence's decision tree shows the possible financial outcomes of each decision and their probabilities, based on Florence's research.

Figure 11.5

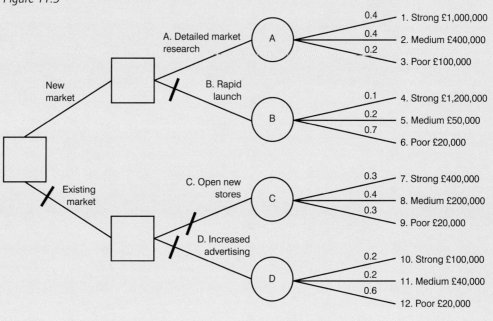

Florence uses the table below to work out the expected value of each possible outcome.

Decision	Outcome	Monetary value of outcome (£)	Probability	Expected value of outcome (value x probability)	Expected value of decision (sum of all possible weighted values arising from this decision)
A	A1	£1,000,000	0.4	£400,000	400,000 + 160,000 +20,000 = £580,000 (node 1)
	A2	£400,000	0.4	£160,000	
	A3	£100,000	0.2	£20,000	
B	B1	£1,200,000	0.1	£120,000	= £144,000 (node 2)
	B2	£50,000	0.2	£10,000	
	B3	£20,000	0.7	£14,000	
C	C1	£400,000	0.3	£120,000	= £206,000 (node 3)
	C2	£200,000	0.4	£80,000	
	C3	£20,000	0.3	£6,000	
D	D1	£100,000	0.2	£20,000	= £40,000 (node 4)
	D2	£40,000	0.2	£8,000	
	D3	£20,000	0.6	£12,000	

Alternative outcomes

Based on this table, the most lucrative single outcome is B1 – moving quickly into the German market (strategy B). This could potentially earn Florence £1.2m. However, taking account of the probability of achieving this success, the expected value of this outcome falls to £120,000. Alternative outcomes from strategy B have even lower expected values; this strategy would actually lose money overall once the cost of the action is deducted from its expected value. Examining all possible outcomes and probabilities for each decision, Florence sees that the strategy with the highest expected value is strategy A (carrying out detailed market research before expanding into Germany), with by far the highest average return. Using decision tree analysis only, Florence would choose strategy A as this has the highest expected value.

⚠ WATCH OUT!

Be careful to distinguish between the most lucrative single chance event and the decision with the highest expected value. Single chance events aren't certain to happen; in making the decision which could lead to this a business also risks less profitable outcomes. Using expected values allow for this risk.

Remember to subtract the costs associated with a course of action from the expected value that you have calculated. This gives the overall net gain (or loss) associated with that decision.

Why are decision trees useful?

● Constructing a decision tree encourages discipline in decision making – it requires analysis and logical thinking. They help to achieve a better understanding of the nature of the decision;

● By considering the probability of each chance outcome as well as potential rewards from it, a decision tree can reduce the likelihood of a business being 'carried away' by a best case scenario which is potentially lucrative but statistically unlikely. It helps businesses to assess outcomes and rewards realistically;

● Decision trees promote quantitative analysis of situations and an understanding of uncertainty. They force businesses to assess the likelihood of negative as well as positive outcomes;

Qualitative considerations

● A decision tree can promote discussion – for example, in exploring the degree of risk which is acceptable to the business, or the relationship between the quantitative outcomes expressed in the decision tree and qualitative factors such as brand image or corporate objectives;

● Decisions trees identify a single 'best' strategy. This can be useful where there are conflicting opinions. They can be used to justify decisions to stakeholders such as managers and shareholders.

Limitations of decision trees as a decision making technique

Data

1. It can be difficult to gather accurate data for forecasting net outcomes and probabilities at each chance node. The data may be to some extent speculative, reducing the usefulness of data analysis and lead to less effective decision making.

Volatility

2. Businesses and their external environment change with time. Some markets are very volatile, especially those reliant on fashion and technology. Decision trees are no use if based on out of date information. A recession may change the economic outlook, making probability assumptions unrealistic; a new competitor may reduce the net outcome of a decision; new legislation may increase costs.

3. The speculative nature of some data used in decision trees means that managers may choose to support particular viewpoints, e.g. by manipulating data to favour a given strategy. Decision-takers need clear protocols for calculating outcomes and probabilities;

Complex strategic decisions

4. Decision trees are most effective when making fairly straightforward decisions with clear monetary outcomes. They may be less useful for complex, strategic decisions which require detailed consideration of qualitative as well as quantitative factors. This is because qualitative issues are not captured in the decision tree diagram. It may also be necessary to consider legal and ethical issues;

5. Where constructing a decision tree is difficult, the resources (time, money, effort) dedicated to this may actually detract from taking necessary action. Costs may rise to the point where potential savings gained by using the decision tree are reduced or wiped out by the process of creating the model.

Show your understanding

1. Each of the following situations represents a complex, significant decision to be made. Work with a partner to discuss whether decision tree analysis would be useful in each situation. If appropriate to the example, sketch out some of the decisions and chance outcomes that might be included in the decision tree:

(a) A private childcare company deciding where to build a new nursery in a rapidly growing city.

(b) Unilever launching a new washing powder.

(c) A large arable farm making a choice about what crops to grow for the coming year.

(d) Sony developing a new product with very high research costs.

2. Mike is a property developer and speculator. A few years ago he bought 5 acres of prime real estate in Thorpe Marriot with the intention of building some new houses. However, the increasing competition in the area has led him to reconsider and he is thinking of selling the land, following his dream, and starting a restaurant in Iceland. If he sells the land now he knows he can get £250,000 and will have to pay the estate agent's fee of £5,000. However he does not know what the market will do and has the option of producing a glossy brochure and waiting six months for the market to improve. This would cost the enhanced fee of £7,000. There is a 60% chance land prices will rise by 30% and a 30% chance prices will remain unchanged. However, there is a small chance (10%) that the market will actually fall by 20%.

Construct the decision tree. What should Mike do?

3. A business wishes to invest in a new factory in order to extend its product range. It has to decide whether to use the factory to make product A or B. Making product A will require a much higher investment (£7m) than the £2m required if they decide to make product B, but the returns look more attractive.

● If A is produced and demand is high (0.7 probability) the payoff will be £16m, whereas if demand is low the payoff will be £6m.

● If B is produced and demand is high the payoff will be £12m. However, there is a 40% chance demand will be low in which case the payoff will only be £4m.

What should the business do?

Major refurbishment at the station

Andrew Hooper is an experienced engineer working for a major multinational construction company. In 2009 he was given responsibility for managing part of the construction project to refurbish the roof of a railway station in London. The total cost of the refurbishment was forecast to be approximately £27m, lasting for 18 months. Andrew's responsibility was to make sure that his part of the project was completed on time and within budget. He had to plan and oversee the removal and replacement of large glass panels from the station roof, 35 metres above the platforms. In conjunction with this he was responsible for water management – making sure that the station stayed protected from rain and snow while the roof was being removed and replaced.

Andrew Hooper on the roof of the London railway station.

All of this was done with the train station still open to passengers while work went on above them.

Planning a major project

The refurbishment plans required many different activities. These included removal of the existing glazing panels and gutters, blasting the steel roof arches to remove 21 layers of old paint back to bare steel, repairing and repainting the arches and installing new glazing panels. 20% of these were solar panels designed to provide around 10% of the power needed to run the station. In order to manage the project efficiently, Andrew had to plan carefully when each activity would take place and the human and physical resources needed for the activity. For example, ordering materials too early would mean high stock levels and poor cash flow management, but any hold up in getting materials when needed could delay the work being done, costing £000's in wasted time.

Part of Andrew's role was to monitor the project over time and to adapt his plan as necessary. For example, the original plan to wet-blast the roof arches had to be changed after the water used began to leak into the station. The replacement method, dry-blasting without water, meant taking extra time to seal the site to prevent dust build-up and to remove the heavy waste generated. This disruption was to be expected: average station refurbishments in London go 70% over budget. This is partly because of the age of the sites, difficulties in getting access to carry out thorough surveys in advance of work and poor maintenance over many decades, due to lack of investment.

Discussion points

1. What difficulties might Andrew have had in forecasting the likely duration of this project?

2. Why might the project have finished late, despite detailed planning?

3. Why is it not desirable for any project to finish after its forecast end date?

The purpose of project planning

As this case study shows, managing a long and complex project is a very challenging job indeed. Without careful management, seemingly small problems at one or two stages can cause knock-on effects which delay the project overall. This can lead to increased costs, damage to reputation and the potential loss of future contracts.

Efficiency

Project planning is a business function which focuses on managing projects so that they proceed as efficiently as possible. Efficiency means minimising waste of resources such as time, raw materials and money. Well planned projects are executed with greater speed and quality, and at lower cost, than those which are poorly planned.

Effective project planning leads to:

● managers having improved understanding of the component parts of the project.

● effective allocation of resources throughout, increasing efficiency overall.

● flexible response to unexpected events during the project.

● increased speed of completion.

Project planning focuses on managing projects so that they proceed as efficiently as possible.

In this chapter you will be introduced to two key tools of project planning: **network analysis** and **critical path analysis**.

> **Network analysis** is the process of breaking down a project into individual component activities in order to identify the relationships between each activity.
>
> **Critical path analysis** identifies the precise sequence of activities that need to be completed within a strict time-frame and the best way to avoid any unnecessary delay.

Construct a schedule

Before we can draw a network diagram it is necessary to identify all of the component parts of a project. This is done in a table, called a *schedule*. This lists each activity, its duration and where necessary, how activities rely on each other.

Individual actions

Example

We can construct a simple schedule showing how to prepare a roast dinner. First, we list the actions needed in preparing the dinner. We forecast how long each action will take. We also make a note of any actions which cannot begin until previous (preceding) actions have been completed.

The schedule for preparing a roast dinner:

	Activity	Duration (mins)	Preceding Activities
A	Roast chicken	100	–
B	Peel potatoes	10	–
C	Roast potatoes	60	B
D	Boil peas	5	–
E	Carve chicken	5	A

This schedule shows us that activity C – roast potatoes – cannot be completed until after activity B – peel potatoes. The chicken cannot be carved (activity E) until after it has been roasted (activity A).

Drawing simple networks

A *network* is a diagram which shows how a project can be broken down into stages and how these stages relate to each other. It is a visual representation of the information shown in the schedule. The diagram has two parts to it:

● *Lines*, which represent activities and their duration. Each separate activity has a different line. The length of the line does not have significance in this diagram.

Nodes

● *Nodes*, which represent the start and finish time of individual activities. Each node is represented by a circle. A network always starts and ends with a single node.

Example

Figure 12.1

The network for preparing a roast dinner would therefore look like this:

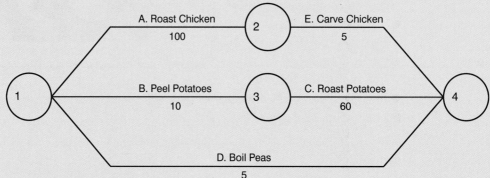

Networks

By analysing a network we can see:

• Which activities rely on the completion of other activities;

• How long is needed for each stage and for the whole project;

• When resources will be needed for each stage of the project;

• The critical path, or those activities which are most critical to the on-time completion of the project.

Remember!

● Activities are represented by lines.

● Nodes represent the start and finish of each activity.

● Nodes are numbered so that each can be clearly identified.

● Lines should never cross.

● Lines should be labelled with the activity (above the line) and its duration (below the line).

● The length of the line has no significance in a network.

● The first node represents the start of the project.

● The final node represents the end of the project.

> A **schedule** is a list of all activities necessary to complete the project, showing their duration and any work that has to have been completed before the next stage can start.
>
> A **network** is a diagram which shows the order and duration of all activities necessary to complete the project.

Calculate EST and LFT

Project managers in business need to know how long their project will take so that they can agree delivery dates with external suppliers. If the project is internal, for example constructing a new production line in a crisp factory, the deadline is equally important so that future business activities can be planned. In almost all cases, others will be relying on the outcome of a project. It is therefore necessary to add further information to the network which shows when the various individual activities and the project itself will start and end.

Earliest Start Time

In constructing a network the first node begins on day 0. This is the earliest time at which the first activity can start. We show this by putting a zero in the top right of the node, like this:

Working through the network from left to right, we can identify the Earliest Start Time (EST) for each activity by adding the EST of the activity which precedes it and its duration. If an activity relies on the completion of multiple previous activities, use the longest or latest of these activities in your calculation. All activities leading *to* a node must be completed before activities leading *from* a node can be started.

Constructing a network

> ### Example
> In the roast dinner example, activity C relies on activity B. B has an EST of 0 (which represents 0 minutes – it can be started as soon as the project begins) and a duration of 10 (representing 10 minutes). The EST of C is therefore 0 + 10 = 10.
>
> Look at the diagram below which shows the EST for all activities. Check that you understand how these were calculated.
>
> *Figure 12.2*
>
>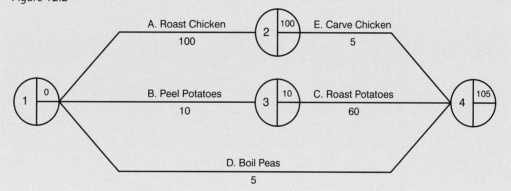

You will see that there is an EST for the final node. This represents the earliest time by which the roast dinner will be completed, or the expected duration of preparing the meal.

For any business project, the EST for the final node represents the expected duration of all tasks. This is the timescale which will then be set for the project, since we can assume that it will be most efficient and desirable to finish as soon as possible. Customers may be given this timescale when placing an order. Internal planning can take place based on the assumption that the result of the project (a new machine or building etc.) will be available for use from this date onwards.

Timescale

In our example, this tells us that it will take 105 minutes, or 1 hour and 45 minutes, to prepare the roast dinner.

Latest Finish Time

If we assume that it is desirable for a project to finish as promptly as possible, we will want it to finish on the EST of the final node. We can say, therefore, that this is also the latest time that we want the project to finish, or the Latest Finish Time (LFT). We show this by putting the same number in the bottom right of the node. See below:

To complete the diagram we now work from right to left, adding the LFT for each activity. The LFT shows us the time by which the activity must be finished in order that the rest of the project is not delayed.

> To calculate the LFT we use the formula: LFT of following activity minus duration of following activity.
>
> **Example**
> In the roast dinner network, activity E has a LFT of 105 and a duration of 5. The LFT of A, which comes before E, is therefore 105-5 = 100. If A finished after the 100th minute it would cause E to finish late, which would then cause the whole project to be delayed.

Avoiding delay

Look at the diagram below which shows the LFT for all activities. Check that you understand how these were calculated.

Figure 12.3

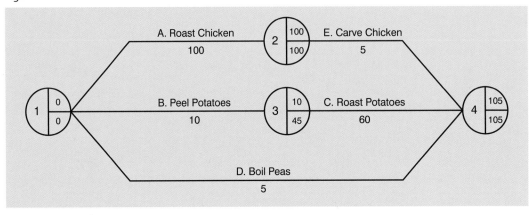

Now that the diagram is complete, a project manager would be able to:

● make accurate predictions about when each activity will begin and end;

● order the resources necessary for each activity at the right time, avoiding additional costs incurred by having resources sitting idle when they are not needed;

Minimising waste

● identify activities which can be completed in parallel, allowing total project time to be reduced;

● reduce capital tied up in the form of resources waiting to be used, therefore improving cash flow.

> ⚠ **WATCH OUT!**
>
> When reading the numbers in each node, remember that the EST refers to the activities following the node (to the right) and the LFT refers to the activities preceding the node (to the left).

> The **EST (earliest start time)** for an activity reflects the duration of all activities which precede it and on which it relies. It is shown in the top right of the node to the left of the activity.
>
> The **LFT (latest finish time)** shows the latest time at which an activity can be completed without slowing completion of the overall project. It is shown in the bottom right of the node to the right of an activity.

Identifying the critical path

You have probably noticed that some of the nodes in the diagram have the same number for both the EST of the next activity and the LFT of the previous activity. Others have different numbers and the EST of the next activity might be *before* the LFT of the previous activity. Where there is a difference, there is some **float time**. This means that the previous activity can be delayed for some time without affecting the completion date of the whole project.

> **Example**
> In Figure 12.3 above, the earliest that the potatoes could be put in the oven (activity C) is after 10 minutes. However, it is possible to delay this until 45 minutes without delaying the meal overall. This means that there is float time for this activity.

Where the EST and LFT numbers in a node are the same, there is no float time and each activity must start and end at a specific time in order to end the project on time.

You will see that the activities without float time form a complete line from the first node to the last. This is called the *critical path*. Activities on the critical path have no float time and directly influence the overall duration of the whole project.

To identify activities on the critical path, it is usual to draw two parallel lines through the activity line, as shown below:

Figure 12.4

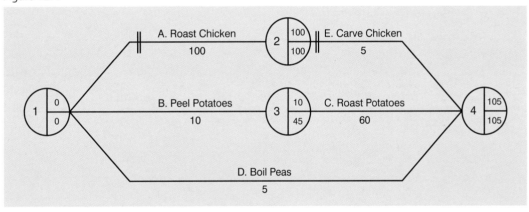

Using information about the critical path

Why is the critical path important? Well, because each activity along it has such a direct impact on the overall project. For this reason project managers may choose to target their attention on critical activities and monitor them more closely than others. They may allocate more resources to ensuring that these activities are completed on schedule, and they would certainly want to know immediately if any of these activities were to be delayed.

> **The roof at the train station**
> Part of the way through the reglazing work, Andrew Hooper (you met him at the beginning of the chapter) recognised that the project was falling behind schedule. This was due to unforeseen damage to roof arches which couldn't be seen during the initial survey. This only became apparent when paint was stripped from the steel frame. The contractors had a target end date. For each day before this that the project was complete, they would earn £25,000. If they finished on or after the end date they would earn nothing. Therefore, it was vital for Andrew to complete his section of the project as promptly as possible. His target was to finish 5 days early, earning £125,000 for the company.

To maintain the pace of the project and reduce delay to the critical path, Andrew and his team reconsidered the shifts allocated to gangs of workers. By scheduling multiple shifts, to work overnight as well as the existing day shifts, Andrew was able to save time and stick to his schedule. Before doing this he had to consider the overtime payments incurred by the nightshifts (which increased costs, but by less than the money lost for finishing later) and the logistics necessary to get the materials needed to the workers who had been drafted in – after all, there's no point having staff on the roof if they've not got any panels available to install!

Calculating total float

We have already seen that some activities have *float time* (you may also see this referred to as 'total float'). This means that their start can be delayed by a certain amount of time without delaying the project overall. To calculate the float time for an activity, use this formula:

Float time = LFT of activity – duration of activity – EST of activity

(Remember: you find the LFT for an activity in the node to its right, and the EST in the node to its left.)

In Figure 12.4, then, the float time for activity C is 35 minutes. The activity could start as early as 10 minutes (when the preceding activity will have finished), but it doesn't have to be completed until 105 minutes (when the project will be complete). Since the activity only takes 60 minutes, it could actually start after 45 minutes and still finish on time – the float time of 35 minutes is calculated as 105-60-10. This shows the difference between the latest possible start time (45) and the earliest possible start time (10).

All activities which do not sit on the critical path will have some float time. Not all activities will have the same float time, so watch for those where the float time is short as these are less flexible than those with longer float times.

Using the information in the network above, we can calculate the float for each activity:

Activity	EST	LFT	Duration	Float	Critical Path?
A	0	100	100	0	Y
B	0	45	10	35	N
C	10	105	60	35	N
D	0	105	5	100	N
E	100	105	5	0	Y

Using information on float time

A project manager will want to allocate resources efficiently. Using float time effectively may mean that an activity is delayed until labour is freed up by the ending of another activity. Alternatively, fewer resources may be allocated with the acceptance that the activity will take longer to complete (though still within the limits of the LFT identified). If activities on the critical path are delayed for any reason, resources may be diverted to these from non-critical activities so that overall timings are not affected.

> **Float time** represents the 'spare time' available for an activity. This shows the duration of time by which an activity can be delayed without slowing completion of the overall project.
>
> The **critical path** highlights those activities for which there is zero float time within a project. Any delay to these activities will delay the project as a whole.

Limitations of network analysis and CPA

The quality of any network will depend on the accuracy of the data entered into it. Where a project is 'new', it may be very difficult to make accurate predictions about each activity. Think, for example, about the Crossrail project in London. How would *you* set about identifying the activities needed to excavate

Adapting to unexpected changes

Flexibility

Using float time well

miles of tunnels under a city of 10 million people? Projects which are essentially repeats of previous works, such as the building or refurbishment of retail outlets, may be easier to plan. However, there is always the need for accurate estimation of each activity and its duration, and the skill involved in this should not be underestimated.

It can be very difficult to construct a network for a large, complicated project. Imagine, for example, all of the separate activities involved in the building of the Olympic Park before the London 2012 Olympics. Computers have made this task much easier, and it is now possible to use project planning software which allows project managers to 'zoom in' on different parts of the network. This allows detailed analysis of component parts as well as a wider overview.

Updating the network

The requirements of a project are not always set in stone. Even once a project has begun, timescales may change for individual activities, or there may be unexpected delays or even changes in the overall project requirement. Some qualitative factors cannot be accounted for fully in advance, such as the impact on large building projects of weather conditions. For network analysis to be useful, therefore, networks must be updated regularly and a new critical path may emerge.

As with any management tool, CPA and network analysis rely on the skills of the person interpreting the information generated and the actions taken as a result. A manager who identifies the critical path, focuses resources on this and ensures regular checks are in place to monitor activities, will have more success than one who commissions network analysis but then does little with it, or makes poor judgements based on the findings.

Effective management

Finally, while a network can be of great use in the oversight of a project and the timing of each activity, it does not guarantee the quality of work within each activity, or that human, financial and physical resources will be available when they are needed. Project planning therefore works most effectively when there is careful liaison between individuals responsible for operations, human resource management and finance as well as the overall project manager.

Show your understanding

Consider the schedule and network below. This shows the main tasks needed to construct a new storage facility for dairy products at a growing farm in Yorkshire.

	Activity	Duration (weeks)	Preceding Activities
A	Dig foundations	6	–
B	Drain site	5	–
C	Construct building frame	2	A, B
D	Complete external walls	10	A, B
E	Build and seal roof	7	C, D
F	Insert windows/doors	3	E
G	Seal floors	4	F
H	Complete internal woodwork	3	G
I	Install and test air conditioning systems	5	G
J	Plaster and decorate	5	H
K	Install equipment	3	J

(a) Copy this diagram and fill in the EST and LFT for each activity. You should find that the project takes 41 weeks in total.

(b) Identify and label the critical path.

(c) Calculate the float time for each activity not on the critical path.

(d) Analyse the likely benefit of carrying out network analysis before beginning to build the new storage facility. *(Answers on page 32)*

Short-termism

In November 2015 Barclays produced a report titled 'Short-termism in business: the long and the short of it' which looked at current attitudes towards short-termism and the potential consequences of focussing too much on the short term. In the report Greg Davies, Head of Behavioural Finance, suggests that people tend to focus on solving today's problems rather than taking a long-term view, and this influences the strategies followed by decision makers in business. Davies says that to overcome this, businesses need to *"pause, just for a moment, and look up at the far horizon. Otherwise what you find is that we are constantly operating in reactive mode."*

In the report, 82% of businesses asked said short-termism affected their ability to think and plan for the long term. The problem is that there is no collective view of what the definition of short versus long term actually is. Smaller companies, it could be argued, have a much more immediate definition of short term because they do not have reserves to sustain them and therefore tend to think in terms of months. For larger businesses, 54% said short term meant the end of the year. Similarly a quarter of small businesses see 12 months as long term, whereas larger businesses see long term as five or so years into the future.

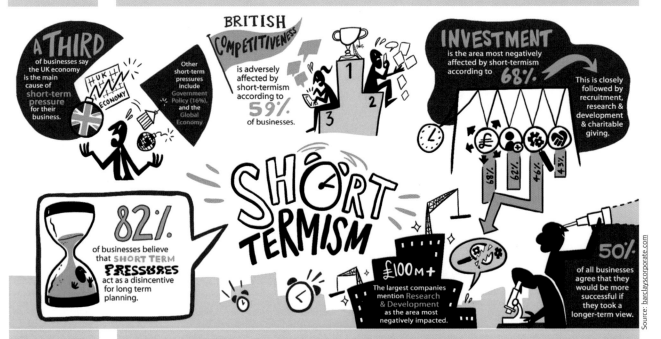

Source: barclayscorporate.com

Shareholders

External pressures

Interestingly the report also looked into the causes of short-term pressure. Within many businesses there is considerable pressure to maintain positive relations with shareholders. The Barclays report said one third of businesses asked see the UK economy as a source of short-term pressure. A further 16% mentioned government policy and 14% suggested it was influenced by the global economy.

Finally the report looked at whether short-termism was predominantly a UK phenomenon. The research suggested that countries which take the longest-term view when making business decisions were Germany, China and the USA. The UK, France and Japan were seen as too short-term focussed.

Discussion point
To what extent do you think the attitude of the leader dictates the strategic decisions the business makes?

Corporate timescales: short-termism versus long-termism

Corporate timescale refers to the implementation of strategies with a built-in expectation as to when returns will be achieved and the strategy can be measured in terms if its success. Of course it is not always

Corporate social responsibility

that easy and the reality is that businesses will have an almost constant stream of urgent and pressing influences, all of which need decisions to be made. This urgency together with turbulence in markets will vary from industry to industry, but will still make it difficult to focus on long-term developments. For this reason the pursuit of quick rewards (or even damage limitation) may push activities that do not pay back immediately to the back of the queue. At the same time, businesses which take a long-term view, especially those that also reflect on ethical issues and **corporate social responsibility (CSR)**, are often seen to be 'better' or 'safer' businesses and therefore more attractive to investors.

> **Example**
>
> **Shazam**
>
> In 2002 users of Shazam would dial 2580 on their mobile phone and hold it up to music. They would then receive a text message telling them the song title and name of the artist. By 2016 the app was used by over 120 million people each month and had 2 billion followers. Andrew Fisher, Executive Chairman said "We define short-termism as taking specific decisions to capture near-term opportunities. In a highly dynamic market there is often a risk of not acting quickly enough. Our longer-term view is based on more significant developments to support our strategy such as moving into a new market segment or developing new technology. Given the investment levels and the time to develop these we take a very considered approach to qualify opportunities."

> **Short-termism** refers to the tendency of many businesses to focus on making a quick profit rather than making plans for long-term growth and development.
>
> **Corporate social responsibility** involves paying attention to the needs and preferences of all stakeholders, not just the shareholders who actually own the business. For example it includes customer care, working conditions, pay, product quality and value for money, as well as the impact of the business on the environment.

This debate includes many perspectives. Shazam makes the case for short-termism in a dynamic market with great clarity. Equally, it is easy to find examples of businesses driven by shareholder pressure. If dividends are low and capital gains elusive, they may simply sell their shares and move on. If the business leaders are in line for bonus incentives based on share performance, their temptation to take short-termist decisions will be overwhelming.

Other influences

Confidence

One factor that affects the way a business makes decisions is the size and age of the firm. Larger more established firms which may have survived scares in the past would have more confidence in taking a longer term view without fear of failure. The Barclays report supports this. Their research said 33% of small businesses felt they would no longer be in existence in 20 years compared to just 5% of larger companies. However, 65% of the businesses surveyed said they had not changed their strategy since the 2008/2009 recession, suggesting that confidence in the future is still an overwhelming influence on taking a short-term approach to decisions.

Strategic leadership

The reality of course is that a business cannot over-focus on the short term, but neither should it ignore day-to-day opportunities and threats. Focussing on the short term could mean companies deal with small problems before they become big problems. Companies such as IBM, Motorola and Nokia are prime examples: a focus on the future meant that short term opportunities were snatched away by the competition. Rivals then drove the market in a new direction, causing all three companies to move from a position as market leader to being a market follower. What is needed is *strategic leadership* as opposed to managerial leadership (short term) or visionary leadership (long term). Strategic leadership maintains smooth day-to-day function and satisfactory short term profit, whilst following a strong path with a clear long term vision.

Lego

Example

When Jorden Vig Knudstorp took over as CEO of LEGO in 2004, he turned the company from a much-loved but static and struggling company to what it is today. By working on a new vision, building better relationships with employees and customers, keeping a tight rein on the company finances and allowing employees to make decisions at all levels, he effectively re-vitalised the company. By paying attention to developing business flexibility, capability and capacity (short term factors) he was able to seize upon opportunities as they arose, leading to longer term growth.

R&D

Some parts of the business world are long term by necessity. Amazon and Google spend billions annually on R&D, and biotech and oil exploration companies sink huge amounts of money in developments which do not produce returns for some time. At the same time the world is undoubtedly riskier today. Change is faster than ever, and new technologies can morph markets and products beyond recognition. It makes no sense, for example, for a traditional retailer to invest in new physical locations if their sector is moving towards virtual retail platforms.

Think!

Adi Ignatios, Editor of the Harvard Business Review, said in January 2014 *"The world would be a better place if businesses stopped thinking so much about short term results and focussed more on the long term."*

To what extent do you agree with this statement?

Evidence–based versus subjective decision making

Strategic

Every business faces a never-ending stream of decisions. Some are long-term strategic decisions, generally made by top management, about the overall direction of the business. These decisions may carry a high degree of risk and are often communicated to key stakeholders. Other decisions will be more tactical, either developing plans to implement a strategy, or responding to market change. Tactical decisions often relate to the short term and are made by middle management. Lastly, operational decisions carry the

Tactical

lowest risk and aim to keep the business functioning on a day-to-day basis.

Whatever the level or type of decision, it is important to understand that decision making is a process leading to an *outcome*. Understanding how the decision was made is essential when analysing its consequences.

Decisions can be categorised in two ways:

● those that are based on a thorough consideration of evidence

● those that are mainly influenced by the views and personality of the decision taker and so are more subjective.

Quantifying risk

Chapters 10-12 introduced techniques that aid strategic decision making, including decision trees and financial tools. These approaches quantify risk and return but as with all evidence-based decision making, the quality of the decision is only as good as the quality of the information on which it is based. Could it be, for example, that a manager wanting to pursue a particular strategy, might over-inflate returns or understate costs? While this may be deliberate, it could just as easily be a case of poor quality or insufficient information. For example in 1999, Larry Page and Sergei Brin, founders of Google, tried to sell the company for $750,000 to Excite, one of the leading search engines at the time, but the CEO of Excite declined. Google is currently valued at approximately $170 billion.

Example

Before smartphones dominated the mobile communication industry, Motorola was an important and influential business. Its strategy involved focussing on the physical shape of the phone, rather than customer experience. Its Razr phone at one point had a 20% market share. However the company misjudged the emergence of smart technology, allowing Apple and Blackberry to exploit the niche. Over a three year period from 2006 to 2009, Motorola lost 90% of its share value. Since then the company has been owned by Google and sold on to Lenovo.

Hunch decisions

It is very important to think about the context surrounding the decision when analysing the motivation behind a particular strategy. A small start-up business which is struggling for survival is likely to be short-term in its outlook. A sole trader with unlimited liability is likely to have a very different attitude to risk from the CEO of a listed company. However don't assume that larger businesses automatically make more considered decisions than small ones. When Fred Goodwin was CEO of Royal Bank of Scotland he made what is now considered to be an ill-advised purchase of the Dutch bank, ABN AMRO. This certainly contributed to RBS having to be taken over by the UK government in 2008. However at the time Fred Goodwin was riding a wave of apparently good decisions, and had a reputation for strong and astute management. Perhaps sometimes managers think that they are infallible, and that their hunch decisions are just as accurate as considered, evidence based decision making. In a fast moving, competitive industry, managers may need to weigh up the time taken to gather scientific data for an informed decision against the speed with which the decision needs to be taken, and, more importantly, the consequences of not seizing the opportunity.

Overall, therefore, it is important not to fall into the trap of thinking short-termism = bad and long termism = good. In reality, the time and energy a business puts into following a long term plan will undoubtedly be affected by the immediate issues and challenges the business faces. However businesses that understand the objectives of their different stakeholder groups may find it easier to follow a strategy which aims for long term growth rather than short term gain.

Example

JCB and Ikea

Ikea

Since 1943, Ikea has offered low priced home furnishing and accessories by following the vision to *'Create a better everyday life for many people'*. Their commitment to product design, consumer value and continuing innovation is shown in their marketing statement which reads *"Your partner in better living. We do our part, you do yours. Together we save money."* Ikea now welcomes over 590 million customers per year globally and has a range of nearly 10,000 products.

The company uses over 1,000 suppliers in more than 55 countries, but their aim is always to build and develop long term relationships. Ikea commits itself to cultivating positive relations with suppliers and follows a strategy of buying product quantities that allow for flexibility. For example they will order 10,000 hours of production from a supplier rather than a fixed number of items. Ikea then ensures a steady supply of raw materials and will even provide financial assistance to suppliers in times of need. This allows Ikea to achieve economies of scale and offer very competitive prices. Ikea has a clear Corporate Social Responsibility (CSR) strategy and a growth target of doubling sales within the next five years. It opens 10-20 new stores per year; a strong focus on the long term means Ikea is robust but flexible enough to survive short term pressures.

JCB

JCB, by contrast, attributes its ability to focus on the long term to its ownership. The construction vehicle manufacturer is one of the UK's biggest privately owned companies. The company is still owned and run by the Bamford family, led by Lord Anthony Bamford (JCB stands for Joseph Cyril Bamford, who started the company in 1945). It has 22 factories and employs 12,000 people. In 2013 JCB had sales of £2.68bn and a profit margin of over 11%. Some analysts have said that by staying privately owned the company can take a long term view towards investments. Mark Turner, Group MD said "We don't have to worry about quarterly results to see what some analysts have to say about us."

When Turner talks about the £150m expansion plan he says "If we'd been a plc, investors would have asked 'What are you doing this for?' It's our business, our responsibility, so let's make the right investment."

The company is now the third largest manufacturer of its kind in the world, behind Caterpillar in the UK and Japan's Komatsu. JCB has a long history, but Turner is more focussed on looking forward rather than backward. "This isn't about yesterday's business," he says. "It's about where we are going to be in five or ten years' time."

Questions

1. JCB invests around 3% of turnover into R&D. How much did they spend in 2013?

2. Contrast the two strategies and discuss which you think is most likely to achieve steady growth over the next five years. Explain your answer.

In September 2015 Matthias Mueller was appointed as CEO of Volkswagen AG, following the resignation of Martin Winterkorn, after it was revealed that Volkswagen had installed emissions test cheating software in up to 11 million of its diesel cars. A newspaper report at the time said that if Volkswagen were to regain the public's trust, Mueller had to "tackle the company's culture" and change what was seen as "a culture of arrogance".

Discussion points

What do you think is meant by 'a company's culture'?

Why do you think a 'culture of arrogance' may have lead Volkswagen to try and cheat the emissions tests?

Corporate culture

Corporate culture refers to the set of important assumptions that are shared by people working in a particular business and influence the ways in which decisions are taken there. It is sometimes expressed as 'It's the way we do things around here'. Every business has a different culture which has been influenced and shaped by a number of factors; it is not just dependent on one person or group. Businesses with a strong and healthy culture are more likely to be successful than those without one.

Strong cultures

A corporate culture is strong when employees believe in the values expressed and actively support and promote them. There are many advantages to having a strong culture. According to James L. Heskett, Professor of Business Logistics at Harvard University, culture *"can account for 20-30% of the differential in corporate performance when compared with culturally unremarkable competitors."*

- Employees believe in the culture and tend to be more motivated because they feel part of the business and involved in its success.
- Greater motivation is likely to lead to increased productivity and better relations with suppliers and customers.

Communication

- There is a feeling of being part of a team, a stronger identification with fellow workers, leading to increased commitment.
- Staff loyalty is higher and staff turnover reduced because employees are more content in their role.
- With everyone in tune with the goals and aspirations of the organisation, communication flows more freely. In turn this encourages greater flexibility.
- Employees are more likely to be innovative and actively seek solutions to problems.
- There is less need for close supervision and detailed policies and rules because the culture is known and accepted by all.

Weak cultures

- Employees have little or no interest in the culture and regard their employment as 'just a job'.

Productivity

- There is little incentive for staff to be creative or make an extra effort.
- Motivation is likely to be poor and this will have a correspondingly negative impact on productivity.
- There is a danger of a rift developing between employees and management, an 'us and them' mentality.

● The more capable staff may well leave for another more positive business, leaving a pool of less efficient and disaffected employees behind.

● Rules may have to be more clearly delineated with sanctions and supervision in place to ensure compliance.

> **Corporate cultures** cover all those attitudes, customs and expectations that influence the way decisions are made in a particular business.

Stakeholders

The **John Lewis partnership** owns 46 John Lewis shops across the UK, 346 Waitrose supermarkets, an online and catalogue business, a production unit and a farm. It employs over 90,000 staff who are 'Partners'; they ultimately own the business. Employees are directly rewarded for success and receive an annual bonus expressed as a percentage of their pay.

According to the principles set out by founder John Spedan Lewis...

● The Partnership's ultimate purpose is the happiness of all its members, through their worthwhile and satisfying employment in a successful business.

● The Partnership aims to deal honestly with its customers and secure their loyalty and trust by providing outstanding choice, value and service.

● The Partnership aims to conduct all its business relationships with integrity and courtesy and to honour scrupulously every business agreement.

In the Verdict Customer Satisfaction Awards John Lewis was voted best retailer in 2013 and 2014 and gained second place in 2015.

Tesco is the UK's largest supermarket and the second largest retailer in the world by revenue. In 2014 an accounting scandal erupted after it was accused of inflating its profits by over £260 million. The scandal wiped more than £2.5 billion off its market value. This prompted an investigation by the Serious Fraud Office. Following this, Tesco's Chairman Sir Richard Broadbent stepped down, eight of its senior executive team were suspended and a new CEO, Dave Lewis, was appointed.

Voluntary codes of practice

In 2015 Tesco's suppliers rated the retailer as the worst of the major supermarkets at complying with a government-backed industry code designed to protect manufacturers. In 2016 the groceries code adjudicator (GCA), said Tesco had seriously breached the legally binding code governing the grocery market and ordered Tesco to make "significant changes" in the way it deals with suppliers.

Customers have been upset by cuts to loyalty cards and staff have been upset about cuts to overtime payments, despite a pay rise of 3.1%. In early 2016 managers were instructed to be 'nicer' to their employees.

1. Using examples from this case study and your own research, assess the corporate culture of both The John Lewis Partnership and Tesco.

2. To what extent do you think corporate culture is responsible for the success of a business?

Classification of company cultures

Charles Handy, a business guru, suggested a way of classifying cultures depending upon certain key characteristics. Seeking to discover where power lies within organisations, he defined four different types of culture – **power**, **role**, **task** and **person**.

Power culture

Within a **power culture**, power is concentrated in the hands of one person or a few individuals. Handy describes the power culture as a 'web', with the power concentrated at the centre and spreading out through the institution. By their nature, power cultures are often autocratic. The leader or leadership makes the decisions; others are unlikely to be involved. There will be few established rules and policies; the leadership will formulate policy as it is needed. One advantage of this is that decisions are made rapidly; this can be useful in a dynamic market. Employees will focus on pleasing the boss, but may become de-motivated at the lack of involvement and opportunities for creativity.

Role cultures

Role cultures result in well-established organisations that tend to be bureaucratic in nature with set rules, procedures and policies. Handy described them as being like a Greek temple, the apex of the temple is where the decision making takes place. The pillars of the temple reflect the ordered units of the organisation which feeds information to the apex and then implements the decisions that come back. The culture will be hierarchical in nature and unlike the power culture, slow moving and cautious, to avoid getting caught out when rapid choices are needed. Leadership may be paternalistic in style; there is little in the way of delegation. Because of its bureaucratic nature,

Charles Handy described role cultures as being like a Greek temple.

employees know and understand their roles. Action beyond the job description is not required or encouraged. There is a danger of the organisation becoming too set in its ways and failing to innovate or move with the times.

Task cultures

Task cultures predominate when the organisation creates teams that focus on a particular task within the broad remit of the overall aim of the business. Handy saw this type of culture in terms of a net or lattice where power and authority lies with the teams. The teams themselves are temporary and consist of employees with the necessary skills and expertise. Once their purpose has been achieved they are disbanded; the personnel join new teams and tackle other tasks. This flexible culture works well in dynamic markets as teams can be assigned to meet new challenges or solve problems as and when they occur. Leadership tends to be democratic and motivation high amongst team members as they have the responsibility to pursue their goals.

Person cultures

Person culture – here it is the individual who matters; the organisation is simply a vehicle through which each person is able to work. It exists solely to meet the needs of its members and has no formal hierarchy or structure as such. It is a loose organisation with individuals that share common abilities and skills. Members are self-motivated, professional and can work with little or no supervision. Such cultures are usually found in partnerships such as accountants or lawyers.

There are some problems with Handy's ideas, the main one being that different cultures may develop within the business. The marketing department may have a role culture, whereas the finance department may have a power culture. With several different cultures in one organisation, it would be very difficult to suggest that the entire organisation has a specific culture. It may also be that a business has no obvious characteristics that will enable it to slot into one of the four types of organisational culture.

> **Show your understanding**
>
> Consider three possible ways in which VW might seek to change its culture. Use examples from other businesses as a way of contrasting the possibilities.
>
> Around 2001, Google's founder, Larry Page said *"We have a mantra: don't be evil, which is to do the best things we know how for our users, for our customers, for everyone. So I think if we were known for that, it would be a wonderful thing."* Would this approach suit VW? Explain.

How corporate cultures are formed

Many different influences shape a corporate culture and it may take a long time to evolve. Each business is different in the way that its particular culture has been created and moulded. Businesses producing similar products or services can have very different cultures.

Cultures are a bit like cooking, the end result depends on the ingredients involved, how they are combined and the processes they undergo. There are many different ways of explaining how cultures evolve but there are some common factors...

● A **vision** may form the basis of the culture, its underlying ethos and its reasons for existing. A genuine and authentic mission statement may set the values of the business and influence the way employees make decisions.

● **Values** are at the core of the company's culture. These will be shaped by the vision, offering a set of guidelines on behaviours and attitudes needed to achieve that vision. Values will affect the way that the business regards its customers, staff and other stakeholders and determine its ethical and professional standards.

● **Practices** become established as the company translates its values into actions. Without application, values become meaningless. Online retailer Zappos.com has ten core values which employees are expected to use in their everyday work. When they are hired, they sign contracts saying they understand the values, and that they can be fired if they fail to live up to them.

● **People** – employees – are at the heart of every successful culture. They need to be willing and able to embrace the values of the company. Many top businesses will actively recruit people who fit in with the culture as well as having the right skills.

● **History** – Every business has a unique history which builds an image over time. It may be exemplified by individuals who have shaped the business, such as Steve Jobs at Apple, or Sir Richard Branson at Virgin. It may come from brands or symbols such as Coca Cola, which makes much of its heritage, or Ferrari and its motorsport background. It may come from past achievements or creations such as Disney.

Difficulties in changing an established culture

Changing an organisational culture is notoriously difficult. Cultures evolve from numerous different areas. The values and practices embedded in the business will have been further shaped by subsequent events. The older and stronger the culture, the more difficult it will be to change it, particularly if it is still seen as successful. 'If it ain't broke, don't fix it' may be the prevailing attitude. People who are used to working in a particular way and are comfortable in their roles are likely to be resistant to change. It is part of human nature to be suspicious of change; some people find it profoundly unsettling.

Cultures may require changes for two main reasons, internal problems and external forces, sometimes both at once. Internally, declining profitability or losses may make shareholders unhappy and wanting better returns on their investments. Externally, customers may become dissatisfied with the products or services offered. New, more attractive, rivals may tempt them away and loyalty is lost.

"I like change, but only a bit at a time."

Example

New ownership, after a takeover or merger, may lead to change. Morrison's took over the chain of Safeway supermarkets in 2004. This looked like a good strategic move; Morrison's had strength in the north of England and Safeway in the south. However, following the £3bn takeover Morrison's ran into huge problems and recorded its first ever loss of £313m. Most of the problems centred on the clash of cultures, Morrison's had a predominantly power culture and Safeway a role culture. The difficulties arose while a new culture was developing, one that would work for both sides.

Innovation

External events may also create a need for change; a successful business may ease up once it is established, only to find a more ambitious and innovative rival overtaking them.

Example

At one time Nokia was the market leader in smartphones. But it failed to develop and innovate fast enough; by 2009 Samsung and Apple were far ahead. A similar fate befell Kodak, the film and camera business, despite its being an early pioneer in digital cameras. In the 1990s Kodak was rated as one of the top five companies in the world; in 2012 it filed for bankruptcy. Analysts blamed the 'culture of complacency' that came from its near monopoly. Kodak still exists but in a much reduced and changed form.

Cultures may need to change when the external environment alters. This was examined in Chapter 4 using PESTLE analysis. Any PESTLE factor may necessitate a change of culture.

Find out

Examine the recent history of Tesco, Barclays and Sony. They have all replaced their CEOs in recent years.

Explain why this is seen as an important step in changing a corporate culture.

Assess how successful this has been for these companies.

Exam style question

Google is well known for its search engine but it also has other projects. Called 'moonshots' within the company, these ventures are wide ranging. Some have been abandoned as unrealistic; others have potentially huge global impact. The best known may be the driverless car. Calico looks into age related decline, Project Wing is developing delivery drones and Project Loon aims to bring internet access to everyone by creating an internet network of balloons flying through the stratosphere.

Big Spaceship is a digital marketing agency, renowned for the cutting-edge web sites that it developed to market major Hollywood movies and leading consumer brands. At Big Spaceship there is no creative department; everyone contributes, everyone has ideas and everyone has a voice. Unlike many traditional agencies, they do not have rigid hierarchies. Every discipline contributes.

Ingvar Kamprad founded **Ikea** in 1943 as a mostly mail-order sales business. The first store was opened in 1958, while the first stores outside Sweden opened in 1963. As of March 2016, Ikea owns and operates 381 stores in 47 countries. Kamprad has kept tight control over the business and his personal ethos has influenced the company's cost conscious approach. Kamprad drives a 15 year old Volvo and always travels economy class, despite being one of the world's richest men. He retired from the board in 2013 and his youngest son Mathias Kamprad took over. Mathias and his two older brothers, who also have leadership roles at Ikea, work on the corporation's overall vision and long-term strategy.

In May 2014 **Asda** decided to shake up its entire store management structure. The grocer is creating 5,000 new store roles to replace a whole tier of middle-management. Of these, 3,500 will be section leader roles with fewer responsibilities and lower pay than the current managers hold. The result will be a new, more centralised structure with online business at the core. Asda is moving control away from stores and delivering centralised control so that staff in stores are little more than implementers.

For **each** of these case studies:

Explain how they might fit into Handy's classification, giving your reasons. *(4 marks each)*

Assess the advantages and disadvantages of that culture. *(6 marks each)*

Chapter 15

Shareholders versus stakeholders

Aston Martin

The luxury carmaker has announced that it will open a new factory in South Wales, creating more than 750 jobs. The new factory will be built in St Athan in the Vale of Glamorgan following a worldwide search for a new manufacturing facility. The plant will be Aston Martin's second factory and will create an estimated 1,000 jobs in the wider supply chain and local businesses.

Discussion points

Make a list of as many groups as you can think of who will be affected by the building of the new factory.

For each group briefly explain the main impact.

Is the impact always positive? If not, why not?

Internal and external stakeholders

Stakeholders are all those people or groups that have an interest in the actions of a business. They include owners, employees, customers, suppliers, lenders, competitors, the local community, pressure groups and the government. Some people identify the environment as a stakeholder.

Stakeholders are further subdivided into two groups, internal and external. Although definitions vary slightly, internal stakeholders are those within the organisation and most directly affected by it. External stakeholders are those outside of the day-to-day running of the business but still affected by its actions.

Internal Stakeholders	External Stakeholders
Internal Stakeholders can influence and can be influenced by the success or failure of the business because they have a direct and vested interest in the business. They are sometimes referred to as primary stakeholders.	External Stakeholders do not participate in the day to day running of the business but are affected by its actions. They deal with the company externally. Sometimes referred to as secondary stakeholders.
Employees: the group of people who work for the company, for remuneration. **Owners**: whoever owns the business. They can be individuals, partners or shareholders. **Board of Directors**: the group of individuals who run a limited company. They are elected by the shareholders at the AGM (Annual General Meeting). **Managers**: people who manage the business and control its day-to-day affairs, e.g. the sales manager, production manager, and the CEO (Chief Executive Officer). This person and other paid senior managers may or may not own some shares in the company.	**Customers**: those who are going to buy the product or service. **Creditors/investors** are individuals, businesses, banks or financial institutions that have provided funds, either short or long term. **Suppliers**: those that provide the business with raw materials or inputs of any kind. **Competitors**: the rivals who compete with the business for resources and market share. **Local community**: people in the area around a business can be affected by its actions. **Pressure groups** are concerned with some specific actions of the business e.g. Greenpeace and the environment. **Governments** ensure that a business complies with legislation and contributes tax revenue.

Employees

Owners

Customers

Don't forget that an individual can belong to more than one stakeholder group. A manager might also be a shareholder in the business, live in the local community and be a consumer of the products made.

Stakeholder objectives

Each stakeholder group has a different interest in the business; it follows that their objectives might also be different. Differing objectives may cause conflict between the groups. Employees might want a pay increase; this will increase costs and may reduce the levels of profit sought by the owners of the business. Stakeholders may also hold the same objectives but have different reasons for doing so. For example, Aston Martin may have moved to South Wales in order to achieve higher productivity and profitability but the local community will welcome the move because it provides employment.

Stakeholder	Main aims of stakeholder
Employees	• A safe and secure job • A good level of remuneration and holiday time • Good working conditions • Rewarding and satisfying work
Owners	• Long term survival and success of the business • A growth in profits • A worthwhile return on investment • Rising share prices and dividends for shareholders
Directors and Managers	• Similar to employees • Other benefits such as share options, private health care, pension schemes and other fringe benefits
Customers	• Good quality products and services • Low prices or value for money • Good customer service during and after purchase • Innovation and choice
Creditors/investors	• Good return on investment • Prompt repayment/payment within agreed trading terms
Suppliers	• Positive working relationship • Fair prices and trading terms • Prompt payments
Competitors	• A competitive advantage over the business • Increased market share • Reduction in competition
Local community	• Increased employment; a positive effect on the community • Reduction in externalities such as noise and pollution • Improved infrastructure • Protection of the environment
Pressure group	• Depends on the cause involved: it may be protecting the environment, campaigning for better working conditions, sustainable production, an end to child labour etc.
Government	• Successful businesses that help to reduce unemployment and contribute to GDP growth • Sources of tax revenue • Higher exports or reduced reliance on imports i.e. a smaller international trade deficit.

Stakeholder and shareholder influences

Stakeholder mapping is a strategic business tool which identifies and assesses the effect of different individuals or groups of stakeholders on the organisation. It is a useful way for a business to analyse the influence and importance of its various stakeholders. It helps managers to understand who the key stakeholders are and what they are looking for. This leads towards formulating a strategy to work effectively with the stakeholders and minimise potential conflicts.

Key stakeholders

Stakeholders are recorded on a matrix which plots their level of interest in issues that affect the organisation against the power or influence they possess to pursue those interests. The stakeholders are broadly divided into four groups according to their relative levels of power/influence and interest.

The top right hand square of the matrix represents stakeholders who are key players from the business viewpoint. They are both influential and likely to take a keen interest in what the business is doing. Keeping this group 'on board' should be a priority for the business; unless they are looked after they are likely to have the ability and inclination to cause problems. This group may include the owners of the business, majority shareholders, important customers and senior personnel.

The top left hand square consists of stakeholders who are just as powerful or influential but not as likely to take so keen an interest in the business. As long as they are kept informed and not forgotten about, they are unlikely to cause a problem. However, they should not be ignored and they have the potential to be just as problematic as the first group, should the situation arise. This group may include major lenders and government agencies including tax authorities. So long as the business is complying with regulations and performing well, they will keep away and not interfere.

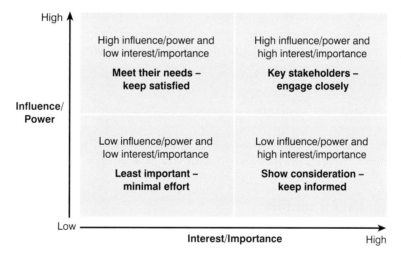

Pressure groups

In the bottom right hand square are those stakeholders who need to be kept informed about the business but only need limited amounts of monitoring and management. They are important to the business but most of the time are unlikely to exert much influence over the actions of the business. This group might include some suppliers, the local community and some pressure groups.

The final, bottom left hand square contains the least important and least influential group of stakeholders. As far as the business is concerned only limited monitoring and attention is needed; they are relatively unimportant and mostly lack the ability to cause trouble. This group might include individual customers or small suppliers.

Every business will have similar groups of stakeholders but they will differ as to the degree of importance and the need for priority treatment, depending on the nature of the business itself.

Show your understanding

BHP Billiton is one of the world's biggest mining companies. Walt Disney is one of the world's biggest entertainment companies.

Think about the stakeholder groups each business will have.

Which do you think are the most important/influential and least important/influential for each company?

Are there any differences?

If so, why do you think this is?

Stakeholder influence

There are two main models that show how a business may interact with its stakeholders, the shareholder model and the stakeholder model.

Shareholder model

> The **shareholder model** focuses on the shareholders and their interests and aims. These are seen as both paramount and synonymous with the interests of the business.

Shareholders are the owners of the business and have taken a risk and invested their capital into the business. As a result, the obligation of the business is to maximise shareholder value by:

● making profits that can be distributed as healthy dividends, and/or

● achieving increased share prices (capital gains).

Other stakeholder groups are seen as being of secondary importance and should there be a clash of interest, the shareholders will get priority.

Stakeholder model

> The **stakeholder model** takes a much broader approach; shareholders are seen as one of many stakeholder groups that the business must consider. This model recognises that the interests of the business are best served by considering and catering for all stakeholder groups rather than just one.

The stakeholder model may have a narrow focus with priority given perhaps just to shareholders and customers. At the other extreme it may be broad in scope and involve all groups. Many organisations will fall somewhere in between.

Employees

Many businesses today make a point of behaving ethically and responsibly. Raw materials may be from sustainable sources; employees may be treated fairly and paid a good wage while customers are given good service and so on. There are advantages and disadvantages to this approach, not least of which is the potential for conflict between stakeholder groups with different objectives and priorities.

The potential for conflict

Ralph Larsen, Chairman of Johnson & Johnson (a major pharmaceutical company) was once asked *"Do you serve shareholders, or do you serve stakeholders?"* His answer was simple: *"Yes"*.

It may seem that looking after the interests and wider objectives of stakeholders is likely to cause conflict with the shareholders who prioritise profit. Safeguarding pay and working conditions for employees, looking after the local community and behaving responsibly and ethically may mean increased costs and reduced profits and dividends for the shareholders. There is a real potential for conflict here. In terms of pure profit, this does not appear to be a profit maximising strategy and some shareholders may well be unhappy about the extra cost incurred by some measures. However other shareholders may see things differently.

Ethical issues

Marks and Spencer have adopted a strategy called Plan A, a long term plan to improve its sustainability and environmental footprint. It is also committed to sourcing its foods and clothing ranges from farms and factories that treat employees fairly and provide good working conditions.

Reputation

If these actions improve Marks and Spencer's brand image and reputation, they may increase sales. More and more consumers are making choices based on ethical criteria and they may be willing not only to choose such products but also to pay a premium price for them. Although short term costs may increase, in the long term increased sales and profitability may not only cancel out the initial costs but increase returns to the shareholders. So conflict may only be temporary and in fact may never happen.

Example

First Quantum Minerals is a mining and metals company which operates in Africa and Europe. It produces copper, copper products, and gold. It does not sell directly to the public and it is unlikely that its industrial clients would be swayed too much by ethical preferences. Yet First Quantum has a strong inclusive stakeholder model that would appear to be in conflict with the priorities of its shareholders.

Community stakeholders

At its mines First Quantum drills boreholes to provide clean water to the communities surrounding the mining area. It helps the local schools and hospitals, improves the infrastructure and runs an HIV/Aids programme with free medical care for all employees and their families. All these measures add to its operating costs, yet the shareholders are happy because the result of this approach is a well-motivated workforce which is productive and loyal. The mines are supported by local communities and governments. By looking after the interests of many stakeholders, First Quantum is also looking after the interests of its shareholders as well.

Exam style question

Mothercare plc is a global retailer for parents and young children. It has over 1,500 stores across more than 60 countries, under its Mothercare and Early Learning Centre brands. In 2015 its sales were £1,203.5m. It is a member of the Ethical Trading Initiative (ETI) and its Code of Practice includes the following points...

- Bribery and corruption are prohibited.
- No forced labour – workers are free to join a trade union.
- Safe and hygienic working conditions.
- No child labour.
- Wages are reasonable and fair with reasonable working hours.
- No discrimination or physical or verbal abuse.
- Environmental impact is minimised with annual targets set to reduce it further.

1. What do you think Ralph Larsen meant when he replied "Yes" to the question "Do you serve shareholders, or do you serve stakeholders?" *(5 marks)*

2. Evaluate the extent to which there might be conflict between Mothercare's stakeholders and shareholders. *(12 marks)*

> *"Everybody from CEOs to shareholders to investors are going to have to be asking themselves not only, 'Is this profitable?' not only whether this will boost my bonus, but 'Is it right?'"*
>
> President Barack Obama

In early 2016 Johnson Controls, an American based company that makes heating and ventilation equipment, decided to merge with Tyco, which has its headquarters in Cork, Ireland. The US corporate tax rate is 35%, in Ireland it is 12.5%. Johnson Controls estimates that it will save $150 million a year in tax.

In February 2016 Carrier Air Conditioning announced that 1,400 American workers will lose their jobs as the company relocates its manufacturing base from Indianapolis to Mexico. Workers there earn about $19 a day, which is less than the American workers earn in an hour.

Why do you think Johnson Controls and Carrier Air Conditioning made these decisions?

Do you think they acted ethically? Explain your reasons.

Moral principles

Business ethics are moral principles that guide the way a business behaves. It is all about doing what is commonly perceived as right rather than wrong. They are nothing new; in the 19th century some entrepreneurs who became household names were guided by moral values. George Cadbury of chocolate fame built Bournville village to look after the welfare of his employees. William Lever, soap manufacturer, did the same with Port Sunlight. More recently Anita Roddick founded the Body Shop with its use of natural ingredients and stance against testing on animals. Bill Gates of Microsoft set up a foundation to enhance healthcare and reduce extreme poverty.

Consumer protection

There are also of course, many examples of unethical business behaviour, almost certainly outnumbering ethical behaviour by some margin. The abundance of investigative consumer programmes on TV, the raft of consumer protection legislation and various regulatory bodies all suggest that unethical behaviour is far too common. Recent cases include the Volkswagen scandal and Scottish Power, which was fined £18m for failing its customers.

> **Business ethics** involve moral principles that determine how business decisions are made. Ethical approaches include providing good working conditions, fair pay and assessment of environmental impacts.

Some aspects of ethical behaviour can be classed as corporate social responsibility (see page 88). There is a grey area between the two. There are times when it can be hard to see the difference between ethical behaviour and enlightened self-interest.

Ethical values are applied to all aspects of business including strategic decision making, relationships with suppliers, employees and customers, marketing and accounting. Behaving ethically takes the business beyond the legal requirements and into the realm of moral values. Both Johnson Controls and Carrier Air Conditioning were acting completely lawfully. Whether they were acting unethically is an opinion and very much depends on what you hold to be ethical or not.

Ethics of strategic decisions

Ethical decision making involves basing decisions on a clearly defined set of moral principles and striving to do the right thing regardless of commercial considerations. It goes beyond corporate social responsibility in a deliberate attempt to behave and act in an ethical manner. This may be based on the individual beliefs of managers but may also be part of the company ethos and culture.

Texas Instruments Incorporated (TI) is a global semiconductor design and manufacturing company. It has a reputation for being a leading ethical company, frequently cited as one of the world's most ethical companies by the Ethisphere Institute, an independent centre of research promoting best practices in corporate ethics and governance.

The company's mantra is 'Know what's right, do what's right'. TI also produces a set of ethical guidelines for all of its employees, which they are expected to follow.

- Is the action legal?
- Does it comply with our values?
- If you do it, will you feel bad?
- How will it look in the newspaper?
- If you know it's wrong, don't do it!
- If you're not sure, ask.
- Keep asking until you get an answer.

Why do you think TI adopt such a strict ethical approach?

Assess the benefits for TI of such an approach.

Ethical guidelines

Many businesses follow a framework to ensure that managers make decisions that are compliant with both company policy and its ethical guidelines. A typical model might have five steps that guide the manager towards an ethical strategic decision.

Step 1 – identify the problem to be solved and any ethical issues it might raise.

Step 2 – gather as much information and data as possible about the problem from as many different sources and perspectives as possible.

Step 3 – identify and evaluate the options based on the best information available and bearing in mind these questions:

- Which option will do the most good or least harm?
- Does this option conform to the existing ethical principles held by the company?
- Am I personally convinced that this is an ethical and good option?

Step 4 – make the decision in the light of moral guidelines and implement it.

Step 5 – review the decision once it has been implemented to see if it could have been improved and note any lessons for the next time.

Trade-offs between profit and ethics

On the face of it there would appear to be a trade-off between profit and ethics; acting ethically may often involve extra costs which would decrease profitability. Sustainable methods are often more expensive and reduce profitability; the most ethical route is not often the most immediately profitable one. Creating and maintaining an ethical policy can be both time consuming and expensive. Systems have to be changed, new procedures adopted and staff have to be trained and persuaded of the merits of being ethical.

Corruption

An ethical stance may mean missing out on lucrative deals and new markets. In countries where corruption is rife the ethical company that is not prepared to offer bribes may not get the contract or necessary permissions. Transparency International (TI) has a clause in its code of conduct expressly forbidding this: "*Do not make, solicit, accept, offer, authorise, approve or promise any sort of bribe, kickback or other improper payments for the purpose of retaining or securing a business advantage.*"

The number of corporate scandals where businesses have been discovered acting unethically, would suggest that for many, profits are more important than ethics. In 2015 the following corporate scandals came to light.

Corporate scandals

- The car manufacturer Volkswagen admitted cheating emissions tests to avoid having to comply with costly regulations.

- The CEO of Toshiba resigned over an accounting scandal that overstated profits by $1.2bn. Investigators concluded that Toshiba's corporate culture was an important factor enabling the emergence of fraudulent accounting practices.

- Investigation into internal Exxon documents revealed that the company's own research had warned of the dangers of man-made climate change as early as 1981. Rather than confront the problem, the company allegedly chose to invest more than $30m (£20.3m) into climate change denial.

The Ford Motor Company is the only carmaker to appear in Ethisphere's most ethical list.

Also in 2015, a report on the US and UK financial services industry by researchers at The University of Notre Dame and the law firm Labaton Sucharow LLP warned that despite the financial crisis of 2008, corporate behaviour had actually got worse and that unethical behaviour was on the increase. The survey was based on interviewing 1200 senior managers. Some of the key points included:

Unethical activity

- One third reported they had "witnessed or had first-hand knowledge of wrongdoing in the workplace."

- Just under half believed their competitors had engaged in illegal or unethical activity to gain an advantage (up from 39% in 2012).

- 30% disagreed with the idea that the financial services industry puts the client's best interests first.

Despite the recent cases above, there is a growing trend amongst some businesses to be more ethical. There have always been ethical businesses but many more seem to be actively following ethical policies and flourishing as a result of it. This may be because of the rise in the use of social media, which is increasing transparency and accountability, and of rising ethical awareness amongst consumers and employees. Research from the Ethisphere Institute claims that firms that rank among the World's Most Ethical Companies outperformed the S&P 500 (an American stock market index) in 2016 by 3.3 percent.

Following an ethical code may well involve higher costs but the rewards may significantly outweigh them. Consumers are more aware of issues such as sustainability, abuse of labour, child labour and the moral arguments for more ethical standards in all walks of life. If this translates into a preference for businesses that follow ethical guidelines then sales may well increase. The Co-operative bank gained many new customers when it launched its customer-led ethical policy in the 1990s. Other businesses have seen great success based on ethical initiatives such as the Body Shop, Café Direct and Patagonia.

Sustainability

Example

The Ford Motor Company is the only carmaker to appear in Ethisphere's most ethical list. Under Executive Chairman Bill Ford, the company has been investing in sustainability. This investment has paid off and Ford has extended its commitment to ethical operations. In February 2016, Ford US sales rose by 18% year-on-year and its European sales also rose 18 percent in the best February performance in six years.

Motivation

An employee who is satisfied with the working environment is more productive than one who is dissatisfied. Unethical practices can cause employees unhappiness, leading to a greater sense of dissatisfaction with the work they do and with their employers. By contrast a strong ethical policy, that is seen to be effective, enhances the motivation of employees and helps the business to be more successful. Satisfied workers are also more likely to stay with the employer, reducing staff turnover and the costs involved in recruitment and training and increasing profitability.

The most immediate impact on Volkswagen following the revelation in September 2015 that it had cheated on emissions testing was a drop in its share price, which reduced the value of the company by 27%; two weeks later it had fallen by 42%. By May 2016 it was still 20% below the pre-scandal level. Having lost investor confidence, companies can struggle to regain the trust of their consumers, investors and shareholders. It may take years to rebuild profitability. A business with a trusted ethical policy may have an advantage in attracting investment, not just from those who actively seek out ethical investments but also from those wary of another 'Volkswagen'.

Pay and rewards

Bonuses and incentives

The area of executive pay is controversial with many top managers receiving very large salaries and lucrative bonuses as well. Bonuses are usually associated with good performance and act as an incentive to managers to work hard and produce the sort of results that please shareholders. Often though, these bonuses are paid despite poor performance. The argument goes that without them, top-class executives would move elsewhere. High levels of pay and bonuses are needed to attract and keep the right calibre of people.

In 2016 The Executive Remuneration Working Group said there was "widespread scepticism and loss of public confidence" over executive pay. The group found that while the FTSE all-share index of public companies was trading at broadly the same levels as 1998, executive pay over the same period had more than trebled.

After the emissions scandal, Volkswagen's supervisory board decided to carry on almost as if nothing had happened. There was a slight decrease, but pay and rewards for the top executives in 2015 came to €63million, down from €70million in 2014. Martin Winterkorn, Volkswagen's CEO who resigned, got a €9.3m termination payment on top of a €7.3m pay and bonus package.

In April 2016 two very different cases of executive pay emerged…

Co-op boss Richard Pennycook took a 40% pay cut and his long and short term incentives were also cut. At the same time 40,000 of the Co-op's shop workers received an 8.5% pay rise. The chairman of the Co-op Allan Leighton, who donates his own six-figure salary to the Co-operative Foundation, said "*The move by Richard to reduce his pay shows the Co-op difference in action, as we champion a better way to do business for our members and their communities.*" The Co-op's profits had dropped 81% to £23m and it struggled to regain its position after the collapse of its banking arm and some tough trading conditions.

BP shareholders voted against a pay package of almost £14m for chief executive Bob Dudley at the oil company's annual general meeting, but the vote is non-binding. This 20% increase was awarded despite a year in which BP reported record losses, cut thousands of jobs and froze its employees' pay. The company had its largest ever loss of $6.5bn mainly due to a collapse in the price of oil and huge fines for the Deepwater Horizon accident in 2011. The company announced it would cut another 3,000 jobs worldwide on top of the 4,000 cuts already announced.

Think!
Why do you think that the Co-op and BP took such different approaches to the pay of their Chief Executives?

What impact do you think these policies might have on other stakeholders?

There have been campaigns to persuade the government to limit executive pay. Assess the possible impact of introducing such regulation.

Corporate social responsibility (CSR)

Ethical values

There is a difference between doing things ethically and doing ethical things. They sound similar but being ethical is about the application of ethical values to all business behaviours and functions. It is about the conduct of individuals as well as the organisation and reflects the corporate culture. CSR is about the way organisations treat their stakeholders, increasing the positive impacts and decreasing the negative ones. This may be through the actions of the business as it follows its everyday operations or through additional voluntary programmes.

A business has four key areas of responsibility...

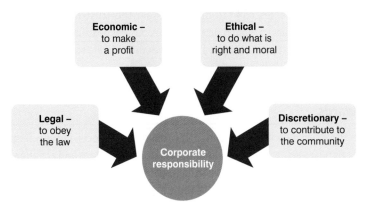

Legal – it must obey the law of the countries it operates in; failure to do so may result in prosecution, although as we have already seen, many companies seem willing to take that risk.

Economic – it must, at least in the long run, make a profit in order to survive. There is also an obligation to shareholders or investors to yield a return.

Ethical – a clear commitment to following ethical policies by the whole organisation. The priority is to act ethically regardless of other considerations.

Discretionary – the business makes a voluntary choice to undertake some kinds of activity to benefit others. This may be by contribution or other means. This is CSR.

Short-term profit

There is controversy over whether a business should follow just the legal and economic requirements, or all four together. Supporters of CSR argue that businesses have much to gain and that they benefit in multiple ways by operating with a wider outlook than their own immediate short term profits. Others simply say that it is the 'right thing to do' and that altruism is part of modern business practice. Businesses operate within society and therefore have a responsibility to put something back into that society.

Critics of CSR say that it conflicts with the fundamental role of a business which is to generate profit. Economics Nobel Laureate Milton Friedman said "...*there is one and only one social responsibility of business, to use its resources and engage in activities designed to increase its profits...*". Other critics argue that CSR is nothing more than window dressing to disguise inappropriate activity or to gain public support.

Revenue and reputation

Undoubtedly CSR does increase the costs of the business. Many of the arguments relating to the shareholder model vs. the stakeholder model also apply here (see pages 82-3). Many businesses hope that their CSR activities will enhance their reputation and boost their revenues as socially responsible customers respond to their programmes. Some companies actively pursue a CSR policy for direct benefits such as cost savings. Reducing waste, being more sustainable and re-cycling as much as possible can bring financial savings as well as helping the environment. Nationwide, the building society, has reduced energy consumption by 15 per cent by making buildings and working practices more energy efficient and investing in new technologies. Calor gas developed an intelligent GPS mapping package to ensure that their vehicles are directed to customers via the most efficient route, reducing distances driven by 1.6 million kilometres per year.

In fact companies undertake CSR for all sorts of reasons; some really do try to be socially responsible because they believe in giving something back to the wider community, whereas for others it is perhaps

Window dressing

just a marketing ploy to make the business look good and increase support. It is certainly true that today, every company from those right at the top of the ethical rankings right down to those at the very bottom all have CSR policies in place.

Question – which company?

This company was recently ranked the 11th best in the world for its CSR work by the Reputation Institute. In 2015 it collected the 'Gold Medal Award for Sustainable Development' from the non-profit World Environment Centre, which praised it for its "understanding of sustainability as a strategic goal and its exemplary implementation." It won the 2014 policy award for Corporate Social Responsibility for its strategic partnership with the Nature and Biodiversity Conservation Union.

Answer – Volkswagen.

In 2016, even after all the revelations had emerged, the Dow Jones Sustainability Index picked Volkswagen as the overall global winner in the auto industry for its commitment to the environment.

Yet, the fact remains that businesses do undertake a huge amount of valuable work that benefits individuals, groups, communities and the environment. These are just a few examples – 1% of Google's equity and profits is donated to appropriate projects, each year it claims to donate $100m in grants, 200,000 hours, and $1 billion in products. The Waitrose Foundation has launched over 450 programmes in South Africa, Ghana and Kenya, focusing on sustainable livelihoods, improved education and health, community development and environmental sustainability. WH Smith PLC is supporting the National Literacy Trust's Young Readers Programme. Between 2005 and 2015 more than 20,000 children could choose around 42,000 free books to keep.

Exam style question

Mothercare – CSR policy

On their website Mothercare aims to… "ensure that we conduct ourselves responsibly, for all our customers, those involved with the manufacture of our products and their communities, and for the environment in which we operate. Our social and environmental commitments go hand-in-hand with being the leading global retailer for parents and young children."

Their CSR programme has four key pillars:

- **Responsible sourcing** – Ensuring that our suppliers and partners treat people with respect and dignity and offer them decent working conditions and pay.
- **Environment** Understanding and reducing our environmental impacts.
- **Our people** – Investing in our people is fundamental to our success.
- **Community** – Engaging with charities and communities.

They are also members of the Ethical Trading Initiative (ETI) and their Code of Practice is based on the ETI's Code.

Questions

1. Explain the difference between an ethical policy and a CSR policy. *(4 marks)*

2. Assess the importance of a CSR policy to Mothercare. *(8 marks)*

3. Do you agree with Milton Friedman's view of corporate responsibility? Explain your reasons. *(10 marks)*

4. To what extent is there a trade-off between profit and ethical behaviour for a business such as Mothercare? *(12 marks)*

Chapter 17

Interpretation of financial statements

The statement of comprehensive income

Imagination

Table 17.1: Financial information from the statement of comprehensive income, £'000

	April 2015	April 2013	April 2011
Sales revenue (turnover)	177,021	151,467	98,045
Cost of sales (COGS)	17,716	20,816	20,791
Gross profit	159,305	130,651	77,254
Operating expenses (overheads)	167,809	119,366	60,994
Operating (net) profit/loss	(8,504)	11,285	16,260
Financial expenses	(3,450)	875	100
Taxation/tax credit	(1,070)	(5,884)	2,918
Profit for the year	(13,024)	6,276	19,278

Source: Company accounts

N.B. Losses are in brackets – they are a negative figure. Tax payments are in brackets, tax credits are added to the totals, so are not. Financial expenses can go either way – a negative figure means a loss and is shown in brackets. COGS stands for cost of goods sold. Terms in brackets are commonly used alternatives that mean the same.

This is what Imagination Technologies Group PLC, based in the UK, said in its 2015 Annual Report:

> *"Imagination has delivered on a strategy of innovation and diversification that has created a globally recognised technology company. Thanks to the long and deep relationships we have with our licensees, strategic partners and our shareholders, we believe the lives of billions of consumers around the world are being enriched by Imagination."*

Imagination supplies other businesses with a wide range of innovative technologies. It describes itself as a global leader in multimedia, processor, communication and cloud technologies. It supplies IT hardware and software. Target markets include mobile phones, mobile and tablet computing, in-car electronics, business networking, telecoms, health, smart energy and connected sensors.

Imagination's customers include Sony, Intel and LG. They patent their discoveries then licence other companies to use their intellectual property – for a fee. Research and development activity account for roughly three quarters of operating expenses. Once they have discovered a good way of doing things, they can licence other companies to use their ideas.

Discussion points

1. Comment on the figures for sales revenue.

2. Explain how shareholders might react to these figures.

⚠ WATCH OUT!

Make sure you have grasped all the work done in Theme 2 on profit and liquidity. You must be comfortable calculating profit margins, familiar with the terminology of company accounts and able to calculate liquidity ratios. You also need to understand the difference between the statement of comprehensive income and the statement of financial position. Revising past work will be really helpful. Don't overlook the section on improving liquidity.

The **statement of comprehensive income** has taken the place of the old 'profit and loss account' in accounting terminology. It shows sales revenue (turnover) and the costs involved in generating that revenue. Cost of sales means the actual cost of creating the output. From these figures you can calculate gross profit – profit after allowing for the direct costs of the production process.

Operating profit

Deducting overheads, (expenses), you then have operating profit – the amount left after all costs have been covered. In Imagination's case, operating expenses are the costs of R&D; the rest covers marketing and administration. Typically, three quarters of Imagination's overheads are spent on R&D.

Operating profit (net profit) is an important figure for any business. It provides investors and owners with valuable information about the viability and health of the company. If it is negative, a loss has been made, and this is a serious warning signal of possible trouble in the future. Losses persisting over a period of a year or more are very worrying, suggesting that it could become impossible to pay the bills. This would lead quickly to insolvency. At this point, strategic thinking might be required. The business would need to look for cost cutting opportunities and ways to increase sales revenue. It may be unwise simply to continue with current operations in existing markets. Action must be taken.

Insolvency

> **Statements of comprehensive income** show sales revenue, costs and profit over a specific period. They may also include tax payable, dividends and retained profit.
>
> **Insolvency** occurs when a business is making a loss and unable to pay all its bills. Typically, the business will borrow for a while but if the losses persist lenders may force the company into liquidation (closing down and/or selling off assets).

Show your understanding and find out

1. Describe Imagination's performance in (a) 2014 and (b) 2015.

2. Looking at the figures, identify the causes of the loss in 2015.

3. Suggest reasons why 2016 figures might be much better than those of 2015.

4. Find the annual report and accounts on Imagination's website and see what actually happened in 2016. Explain possible reasons and probable consequences.

Interpreting statements of comprehensive income

Profit margins

Profit margins can be very revealing. Gross and operating profit margins are sometimes referred to as **profitability ratios**. These can be used by managers, shareholders and potential investors to compare businesses and also to analyse business performance over time.

When analysing profit margin data, keep in mind the way profit margins vary from one business to another. There is a connection between the operating profit margin and the amount of value added.

● Supermarkets add value mainly by providing a sales outlet and will often have relatively low operating profit margins. Much of their turnover is spent buying the goods they supply, paying for their premises and covering staff pay. They can make a good profit with a quite small margin on the sale of each product, if their sales volume is sufficiently large.

● Businesses that actually create a product from raw materials or semi-manufactured components will tend to have relatively low gross profit margins as more of their costs will be incurred directly in the process of production. They will be adding much more value than a supermarket does.

Risk

● Importantly, any business that faces relatively high risks will expect higher profits to compensate for the risks that they are taking. They will be trying to build up reserves of retained profits in case of losses in the future. Oil and mineral exploration is risky – it may be hard to find good sources. So businesses like Exxon Mobil and BP make quite big profits some of the time, but profitability may vary considerably from year to year.

In order for analysis to be meaningful, you have to compare like with like. You can compare profit margins for one business over a period of years, or for several businesses that are producing similar goods or services in the same period. This would provide a sound basis for assessing the financial health of the business.

> **Gross profit** is sales revenue minus cost of goods sold, i.e. labour, raw materials and other inputs that vary with the level of production.
>
> **Operating profit** allows for overheads as well as direct costs. Overheads are all the costs that do not change with the level of output.

Show your understanding

Using the figures in Table 17.1, calculate Imagination's gross and operating profit margins for 2011, 2013 and 2015. *(Answers on page 37)*

1. What conclusion can you draw from these profit margins?

2. Explain two possible causes for concern in these figures.

Stakeholder interest

Dividends

Shareholders want either dividends or capital gains – or best of all, both. In its early, years Microsoft gave no dividends to shareholders. It ploughed all the profits back into R&D and product development. Shareholders didn't care – the shares grew in value so fast that they could not lose. Shareholders in Marks and Spencer would not feel like this – they would probably prefer profits distributed as dividends, rather than business expansion. Clearly, shareholders will look at company accounts to see how the business is performing. If the results are not good they may sell their shares.

Sometimes retained profit is shown in the statement of comprehensive income. This may be invested in future expansion, or if this does not happen, be distributed to shareholders as dividends.

Employees will hope that growth in turnover will bring higher pay. However, they may also be pleased if jobs are created. They may wonder whether the operating profit justifies the managers' pay. Customers are much less likely to be interested in company accounts but suppliers will be very interested in their customer's performance. Orders may rise or fall.

Think!
...about Imagination's stakeholders. Where will they stand on the 2015 figures?

The statement of financial position

Assets and liabilities

The statement of comprehensive income tells us about how the business has performed over a period of time in the past (usually a year). Also very important is the **statement of financial position**. This provides a snapshot of the **assets** and **liabilities** of the business on a particular date. It shows how much money has been put into setting up and maintaining the business and the ways in which the capital has been used. This shows what the business is worth – what it owns, how this has been financed and, therefore, how much value really exists for shareholders.

Limited companies are legally obliged to produce both documents as part of their published accounts. Table 17.2 shows extracts from the statement of financial position for Imagination on April 30th, 2013 and 2015.

Statements of financial position answer two basic questions about a business:

● Where did its resources come from?

● Where are those resources now?

Businesses buy their assets using share capital and any available retained profit together with loans. Managers are responsible for ensuring that the business makes the best possible use of its resources while pursuing the firm's objectives. So owners, shareholders and potential investors want to know just how those resources have been used.

Table 17.2: Extracts from Imagination's statements of financial position, £'000s

Statement of financial position

	April, 2015	April, 2013	
Non-current assets	206,266	189,626	Intangibles include brands and
Of which, intangibles	108,219	114,596	patents
Current assets			
– inventories	7,901	8,512	Inventories are stocks of inputs
– debtors	82,450	64,018	and finished goods. Debtors refers
– cash	2,651	76,572	to money owed to the business
Total current assets	93,002	149,102	
Total assets	299,268	338,728	Current and non-current
Total current liabilities	49,334	96,497	Short term debts
Net current assets	43,668	52,605	Working capital
Non-current liabilities	44,460	50,839	Long-term loans
Shareholders' funds	205,474	191,392	Total equity finance

Source: Company accounts

Net current assets = current assets – current liabilities = working capital

Capital employed = non-current assets + working capital

Intangible assets

Every business has resources that it can use to create and sell products. These are tangible, non-current (fixed) **assets**, including all the buildings, plant and capital equipment that can be used to create output and generate income. They can be valued and recorded in the accounts. Some companies hold shares in other companies, which count as non-current assets. Imagination also has many **intangible assets** (which are also non-current assets). Most of the technologies that it has developed are patented; they are intellectual property, and crucial to the way the business has developed its successful and distinctive products. Other intangibles include goodwill, which includes the customer base and the reputation of the business. Reputation is founded on the skills and ingenuity of the workforce and the management.

Assets

The **statement of financial position** shows how much capital has been invested in the business and how it has been used.

Assets are items of value that bring a flow of benefits to the company.

Current assets include stocks (supplies of inputs or finished products), debtors (the amounts of money owed to the business which will be paid in the near future) and cash (money in the bank. Trade credit offered to customers is included in 'debtors'.

Intangible assets include patents, trademarks and copyrights, all forms of intellectual property (IP), and the goodwill that goes with customer loyalty and repeat purchases. IP has value – unique innovations can be sold or licensed in order to generate income.

The statement of financial position also shows the **liabilities** – the debts that the business will have to pay in the future. It is useful to be able to borrow funds from banks and other sources in order to finance research and investment but growing liabilities could be a warning signal to managers and investors that the business could struggle to repay large amounts.

If you look at other companies' accounts you may find that they are not all set out exactly as they have been in this chapter. You need to be aware of variations in the terminology. The alternative terms in Table 17.1 and the last column on Table 17.2 may help.

Liabilities

> **Liabilities** are all the debts that will have to be repaid sooner or later. **Current liabilities** are short-term debts that will be repaid within one year. They include overdrafts that tide the business over when expenses are heavy and sales revenue will be delayed. The size of the loan will fluctuate month by month. **Trade credit** given to the business by suppliers allows time to pay but is a current liability.
>
> **Non-current liabilities** are medium and long-term loans that will be repaid over a period longer than a year. They include bank loans but could come from other bodies such as venture capital businesses. Long term loans often finance fixed assets.
>
> **Shareholders' funds** represent the money that was originally invested by buying shares (share capital).

Liquidity

Show your understanding

1. What impact would higher R&D spending at Imagination have on intangible assets?

2. Both current assets and current liabilities appeared to be decreasing, even though sales revenue and shareholders funds were rising. Why might this be?

Stakeholder interest

Both the statement of financial position and the statement of comprehensive income will be drawn up by professional accountants. Shareholders and managers will study them carefully because they can reveal so much about business performance. The two documents provide the data for calculating working capital and the liquidity ratios – the current and acid test ratios – and also the performance ratios, covered in Chapter 18. All these provide valuable information on the liquidity and profitability of the business. The figures show how the business will cover its debts and whether it has the capacity to expand in the future.

Investors, bankers and financial advisers will be likely to study the statement of financial position before deciding where to invest their own or other people's money.

Show your understanding

1. Calculate the current and acid test ratios for Imagination in 2013 and 2015.

(Answers on page 37)

2. What do these ratios tell you about the company's liquidity position?

3. In the light of the results, would you recommend a course of action? If not, explain why not.

Chapter 18

Ratio analysis

Imagination's results

In 2013 the Chief Executive commented:

"We have established leading positions in two of the fastest growing global markets – smartphones and tablets. In smartphones we are on course to maintain strong market share, whilst we provide the technology for many of the leading tablets." That year, Imagination bought MIPS, a hardware specialist. It was expected that Imagination and MIPS would complement one another in a number of ways.

In April 2015, the CEO was still optimistic. Imagination had always gone for both organic and inorganic growth. MIPS, the subsidiary, had performed better than expected. However, there were clouds on the horizon. The Chinese market was slowing slightly and a backlog of payments (debtors) had arisen. The company decided to sell another subsidiary, Pure, the DAB radio maker, to raise cash. This happened in early 2016.

Point for discussion

Imagination's M&A activities involved different types of integration. Work out which types of integration applied to the takeovers of MIPS and Pure. (If this seems puzzling go back to pages 30-31.)

How might Imagination have paid for MIPS?

How might buying MIPS and selling Pure affect the figures in the statement of financial position?

This chapter is all about evaluating business performance. Accounting ratios help by highlighting key features of the financial results. In Theme 2, you learnt about the profitability ratios – gross and net profit margins – and the liquidity ratios, the current ratio and the acid-test ratio. This chapter is about gearing and ROCE, the return on capital employed. All these ratios help in analysing business performance.

Gearing

Businesses can fund their investments in three ways:

Retained profit

- using retained profits that have been kept as reserves. The business can plough back these profits, investing to increase income in the future.

Selling shares

- creating and selling shares for cash. If investors are willing to pay a good price for the shares, in the expectation that the business will do well in the future, this works. In return, the business will pay dividends to shareholders but in a bad year, dividends may be kept low or not paid at all.

Borrowing

- securing long-term loans, usually from banks. This is an important source of finance but interest has to be paid every year, not just when sales are buoyant. At some point the loan will have to be repaid. These debts are termed 'non-current liabilities'.

Businesses with very large non-current liabilities (long-term loans) can get into difficulty if their investment projects are not as successful as hoped. The interest burden may threaten their profitability and repayments will have a negative impact on cash flow. So it is important that businesses do not rely too heavily on borrowing. *The gearing ratio measures the extent to which a business us funded by debt.* The formula is:

$$\text{Gearing} = \frac{\text{non-current liabilities}}{\text{capital employed}} \times 100 \quad \text{(Answer expressed as a percentage)}$$

Banks are keen to lend when the economy is growing fast and profits are rising. As businesses borrow more, gearing ratios will rise. But businesses with high gearing ratios may encounter problems if the rate of interest rises because they have to pay more for their loans. Further problems occur if the economy slows and sales revenue falls, because repayments must still be met.

Gearing ratio

The higher the gearing ratio, the more risks the business is likely to face. A realistic gearing ratio might be 50% – anything above that is typically regarded by accountants as high gearing and therefore risky. However, if interest rates are low there might be less reason to worry about increased borrowing.

Low gearing makes a business safer but may also indicate lack of management dynamism. As always, careful interpretation is required, of both the individual business and the business environment in which it is functioning.

> The **gearing ratio** measures the proportion of capital employed which is covered by long-term loans. Excessive reliance on loan rather than share capital is risky.

Show your understanding and find out

Use Table 17.2 (page 93) to calculate Imagination's gearing ratios for 2013 and 2015. (Capital employed is non-current assets plus working capital, but in an exam you will be given figures for capital employed.) Explain the changes. Then calculate gearing ratios for two other businesses, and consider how and why they each vary. *(Answers on page 37)*

Return on Capital Employed (ROCE)

Investing

Most shareholders invest in businesses to earn money. They know that there is an opportunity cost of investing – the missed opportunity to invest their money elsewhere. So they want to be confident that their money is earning as much as possible. ROCE is a financial ratio which tells us about the level of profit earned by the business in relation to the amount of capital invested in it. It shows investors how effectively their money is being used.

$$ROCE = \frac{\text{Operating profit}}{\text{Capital employed}} \times 100$$

In the accounts, capital employed consists of all sources of capital (shareholders funds plus long-term loans plus retained profit). But the simplest way to calculate this is:

Capital employed = non-current assets + working capital

The higher the ROCE figure, the better. If it is rising, it shows that the business is generating more profit for each pound invested in the business. ROCE is an important indicator but has its limitations.

Using ROCE

Uses of ROCE	Limitations of ROCE
• Used by managers when raising debt finance: if ROCE is less than the rate of interest payable on the loan, repayment may be difficult. • Used by potential investors: if ROCE is higher than the returns that could be obtained on possible alternative investments, then the investor will be more likely to invest. • Used by existing investors: if ROCE is lower than alternative investments, shareholders may decide to sell their shares and use their money to generate better returns elsewhere. • Can be used to show trends over time – whether the business is generating more or less profit for each pound invested.	• Isolated figures may not be of much use. Data is most useful where it shows trends over time, or when compared to similar businesses. • One-off events, such as large acquisitions, may reduce ROCE for a particular time period. This could give a negative impression of the business unless the reason for this is made clear.

Show your understanding

1. Use Tables 17.1 and 17.2 to calculate Imagination's ROCE for 2013 and 2015.
2. Comment on shareholders' likely opinion of the ROCE figures. Keep in mind that possible external risks could influence this. *(Answers to question 1 on page 37)*

Efficiency

If ROCE is considered to be too low, managers might choose to take action. This may be an indication that the business could be managed more efficiently. Any measure that will increase productivity, cut costs or increase sales revenue may be useful.

If ROCE is very positive, this might lead to a new growth strategy. Imagination went ahead confidently with the takeover of MIPS because 2012 was a good year and ROCE was high.

> **ROCE (return on capital employed)** is profit as a percentage of capital invested. It reflects the effectiveness with which the business uses its capital employed.
>
> **Capital employed** is the total of all investments, i.e. non-current assets plus working capital.

Interpreting ROCE and gearing

Evidence for banks

Banks will usually consider the gearing ratio before deciding whether or how much they will lend. Especially with a new business, they want evidence that their loan can be repaid. A business which is highly geared may find it harder to repay debts than one with low gearing.

When a business gets a new long-term loan from the bank, both ROCE and gearing will change. Capital employed will increase, implying a fall in ROCE. The gearing ratio will decrease. For the lender, risk increases. One way for the bank to avoid risk is to require collateral for the loan. This could be based on the value of the business premises, but if these are rented then the loan may be secured against the business owner's home (for a small business) or against larger fixed assets. For large and small businesses, a key factor will be the amount of share capital that the business already has. The more assets the business has, the more confident the bank will be about making a loan.

Potential investors also will consider the gearing ratio. They may be wary of investing in a highly geared business if they have concerns about the ability of the business to meet repayments; this could reduce the chance of the investors' realising a good return on their investment.

The limitations of ratio analysis

Interpret ratios in context

Financial ratios have many uses. They can be used *within* the business as a management tool for comparing the profitability of different products. They help stakeholders *outside* the business to make lending or investment decisions. They do not give a rounded picture of the organisation unless examined in the context of the full range of activities within the business. It is important to consider many other sources of information before drawing final conclusions.

● Ratios may be affected by changes in the economy. They need to be viewed in context and interpreted with reference to expectations about the future.

● Both quantitative and qualitative information may be needed to explain the meaning of each ratio. For example, in Table 17.1, Imagination's expenses look very high. That and the very low cost of sales explains why the gross profit margin looks high too. But this is easily explained once you know how much the company spends on R&D.

● Reading the chairman's report would be one good way to get qualitative information to support ratio analysis. Although, for a big business, news reports might show that the chair has been doing some 'window-dressing', perhaps by concealing information which does not suit their purpose. In general the more supporting background information that can be acquired, the more accurate the analysis is likely to be.

● Qualitative information that could be useful might include the ethical stance of the business, how much affected it is by technological change and its strategic planning for the future.

Ratios vary greatly from one business to another; very careful interpretation is required. This in turn means that the person who is interpreting the ratios must be very well acquainted with the business, and the industry, concerned. Ratios can be compared over time for the same business; alternatively in any one year, comparisons can be made with businesses in the same industry and similar circumstances. Remember, though, that ratios do not tell you anything about the non-financial aspects of the business.

Maintaining competitive-ness

For a business where innovation is of the utmost importance in creating a competitive product, the pace and quality of any new technologies under development would be of paramount importance. This would determine the reputation of the company and therefore its future profitability. Imagination could continue to be highly successful, but perhaps only if it has plenty of new and interesting ideas in the pipeline.

In general, reputation and innovation are important elements in determining competitive advantage. Information about competitive advantages that the business can lay claim to will often be significant in any assessment of company performance. Qualitative information that illuminates business activity, examined side-by-side with the financial statements and ratios, can provide a more balanced picture than any one data source alone.

ANSWERS: Page 48

1. (a) Average yearly sales figures = £11.8 million per year.

(b)

Year	Sales (£m)	3 year Moving Average
2006	8	
2007	12	10.00
2008	10	12.67
2009	16	14.67
2010	18	14.67
2011	10	12.00
2012	8	8.00
2013	6	9.33
2014	14	12.00
2015	16	

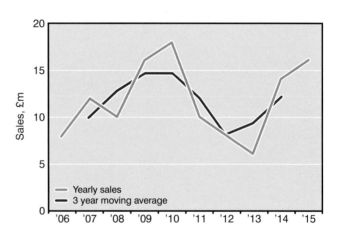

(c) **Analysis** marks will come from identifying trends in the data. At face value it seems the business is cyclical. Sales in 2009 and 2015 were twice as high as in 2006 and 2012. Is the business flexible enough to cope with these changes? **Evaluation** marks will come from discussing whether the move would be in addition to, or instead of, the existing homes? High priced homes may be more vulnerable to economic downturns, but the profits could be greater. Is this sufficient data to make a decision? If not, what else should the business do?

2. (b)

Year	Quarter	Sales (£)	4 Quarter Total (£)	8 Period Total (£)	4 Quarter Moving Average (£)
2012	1	3300			
	2	2200			
			12500		
	3	3600		25100	3137.5
			12600		
	4	3400		27300	3412.5
			14700		
2013	1	3400		29700	3712.5
			15000		
	2	4300		30700	3837.5
			15700		
	3	3900		31600	3950.0
			15900		
	4	4100		32000	4000.0
			16100		
2014	1	3600		33900	4237.5
			17800		
	2	4500		37900	4737.5
			20100		
	3	5600			
	4	6400			

Chapter 19

Human resources

Labour productivity

In a clothing factory in Bangladesh a good wage for a garment worker might be US$5 per day. If the worker can sew 50 items per day, the average wage cost is $5/50 garments = $0.10 per item. If the worker increases their rate of output to sewing 63 items a day, the average cost per item falls to just under $0.08. The worker earns the same but the average cost per garment has

fallen. The clothing producer now has two options. The price can stay the same and profit margins will rise. Alternatively prices can be reduced and profit margins kept constant. In the highly competitive low-cost garment industry in which most Bangladeshi factories operate, this second option would look attractive because sales would probably rise.

⚠ WATCH OUT!

You examined motivation and efficiency towards the end of Theme 1 and productivity and efficiency towards the end of Theme 2. Both are relevant to this chapter. Make sure you have understood both topics.

Cutting average cost

Productivity measures how efficiently resources are used. High productivity involves using resources in ways that maximise output and minimise waste. **Labour productivity** is a measure of the output produced by each employee in a business. Employees must be paid an acceptable wage rate so the higher the output per worker, the lower the average costs of production will be.

Calculating labour productivity

Labour productivity is calculated by identifying the output per worker over a specific time period – per hour, per day or per year. At the national level it is given as output per person per hour worked.

$$\text{Labour productivity} = \frac{\text{Total output per time period}}{\text{Number of workers}}$$

The answer is expressed as output per person per time period, most often output per person per hour.

Example
A bakery produces 1000 loaves of bread per day. There are 5 employees. The labour productivity is

$\dfrac{1000}{5}$ = 200 loaves per person per day

Labour productivity is a measure of how efficiently a business uses its employees to produce output. It is expressed as output per employee per time period.

Show your understanding
Identify one large and one small business that you have come across and that have for some reason had a change in productivity. Explain why productivity rose or fell.

Labour turnover

Staffing

Kevin Baker was worried by the figures in his latest business update. As the Human Resources Manager for a well-known regional confectionery producer, he was in charge of managing 200 members of staff. Kevin had always prided himself on knowing all his staff by face if not by name, but recently his walks around the factory floor reminded him of just how many new staff had been hired lately and how many old faces had gone. The business update figures shouldn't have come as such a shock, then, but somehow it was still a surprise to see that 40 staff had been replaced in the previous twelve months. Kevin got even more of a shock when he saw the bill from a local recruitment agency which he had used to find these replacement staff. If this carried on, his own post might be filled by a new face before long!

Discussion points

What percentage of the workforce was replaced during the year?

What negative consequences might this have had on the confectionery producer?

What factors might have caused these staff to leave?

Labour turnover records the percentage of the workforce represented by employees who leave their jobs and need to be replaced in a year. Since there are costs associated with having high numbers of new staff, it is a general rule of thumb that businesses aim for low, stable labour turnover.

Reasons for leaving

Workers leave their jobs for a range of reasons. Some are unavoidable for the business – parents leaving to care for children, for example, or people retiring as they reach old age. Other reasons might include leaving to start their own business or to get a job with better pay or conditions or opportunities for promotion. Employers may not want to lose these people and can take action to retain them.

Sometimes there are redundancies. There may be a policy of natural wastage, when having a smaller workforce would be helpful. The number of employees can be allowed to fall gradually as people leave. These changes are not included in labour turnover figures since there is no need to replace them.

Labour turnover rates tend to be higher in retailing, catering, call centres, construction and media.

Median labour turnover

A CIPD* report (CIPD 2013) reported that median labour turnover in the UK was just under 12% in 2012. At that point, the economy was just recovering from recession; more recent estimates (2015) suggest an average for the UK of 15.6%. Labour turnover rises when unemployment is low and there are skill shortages: employers may outbid each other to get the people they want.

Labour turnover rates can vary considerably across industries so when interpreting figures make sure you consider what the numbers mean in the context of a particular business and industry. They tend to be higher in retailing, catering, call centres, construction and media. Labour turnover is usually lower in the public sector and legal and accountancy services. Sometimes high turnover occurs because the business is restructuring or re-locating; this would be temporary and of no great concern.

*Chartered Instute of Personnel and Development

Calculating labour turnover

Labour turnover is calculated by comparing the number of workers who leave and are replaced over a time period (usually a year) to the number of employees in the workforce at any one time. It is expressed as a percentage of the workforce.

$$\text{Labour turnover} = \frac{\text{total number of workers leaving in a time period}}{\text{average number of workers employed in that time period}} \times 100$$

Example

In the case study above, we saw that 40 staff left and were replaced, out of a total workforce of 200. Therefore, the calculation of labour turnover for the year is:

$$\frac{40 \times 100}{200} = 20\%$$

This means that over the year, 20% of the workforce left and was replaced. Another way to think about this is that the number of times that replacement jobs were advertised (40) was 20% of the total number of jobs available in the organisation (200).

It is possible for labour turnover to exceed 100%. This would happen where the average worker stayed in their post for less than 1 year. This is much more likely in some industries than others – in retail, for example, and in the fast food industry. This is because the work is low-skilled and the employees are more likely to be students working in school or university holidays, or travellers from overseas who are in the UK only for a limited time. In this case, the number of replacement posts advertised over the year would be greater than the number of jobs available at any one time.

Impact of high labour turnover

New staff may be highly motivated

New staff can bring much to an organisation – new ideas, new skills and enthusiasm – which can motivate those around them. A business with very low labour turnover may actually suffer as a result of not gaining access to new ideas; the business could lose competitive advantage to more dynamic competitors. However, there are also costs associated with labour turnover.

● Recruiting new staff costs time and money – to advertise, to interview and to appoint;

● Training new staff also requires time and, often, money;

● New staff take time to settle in and there may be a loss of productivity while this happens;

● When existing staff leave they take their knowledge and skills with them. These are then lost from the organisation. Worse, they are often gained by a competitor who is then able to benefit from them;

Recruitment costs

● A high rate of staff turnover may suggest that many employees don't want to work there. This could damage the organisation's reputation and make it harder to attract and retain high quality staff in the future.

> **Labour turnover** is a measure of the rate at which people leave their jobs and need to be replaced. It is expressed as a percentage of the workforce per time period.

Labour retention

Retaining skills

The retention rate of an organisation tells us about the stability of staffing in the business. A high retention rate shows that an organisation, or part of it, retains experienced employees over time. Typically, a high retention rate is a positive indicator although, as noted above, some labour 'churn' can be positive in bringing new ideas and skills into a business.

Labour retention is calculated by comparing the number of workers who have been working at the business for a year or more to the total number of employees in post one year ago. It is expressed as a percentage.

$$\text{Retention} = \frac{\text{number of staff with service of 1 or more years}}{\text{Total number of staff in post 1 year ago}} \times 100$$

Example

In the case study above we saw that 40 staff left over the year and were replaced, out of a total workforce of 200. Assuming that, of the remaining 160, 120 have been with the business for a year or more, and that the total workforce size has remained the same for the last year, the retention rate would be:

$$\frac{120 \times 100}{200} = 60\%$$

Notice that the retention rate is not calculated by subtracting the turnover figure from 100 (the labour turnover rate is 20% per year). You must carry out each calculation separately if necessary.

> **Labour retention** measures the proportion of the workforce who have been in post for a year or more.

Absenteeism

Absence is costly

Some absenteeism has a good reason – such as sickness, injury and attending to family commitments. There may also be absenteeism for no good reason. Absence is usually reported as an average per employee per year, either as a % of working time or, more commonly, as the number of days lost per year. The lower the rate of absenteeism, the better. Recent research shows that the average level of employee absence in 2015 was 6.9 days per year. There was considerable variation across sectors with employees in manual, public sector and large organisations more likely to be absent from work. Absence due to mental health conditions such as stress and depression is increasing in many organisations. Employee absence will usually damage business prospects.

● Absent employees cannot complete work, leading to falling productivity and rising average costs. Deadlines may be missed, disappointing clients or incurring late penalties;

● Colleagues may have to 'cover' for absent workers, increasing their own workload. This could lead to poorer quality work, increased stress and resentment;

● Absence can be an indicator that something is wrong within the organisation, causing employees to get ill, injured or demotivated. For example, rising levels of stress-related absence could indicate poor management.

The absenteeism rate is the percentage of employees absent on one day. The average rate can be calculated for any given period by adding up total absences and dividing that by the number of days.

$$\text{Absence rate (\%)} = \frac{\text{Number of employees absent}}{\text{Total number of employees}} \times 100$$

Absenteeism is a measure of the working days lost each year due to employees being absent from work. It is expressed as a % or an average number of days lost per employee.

Show your understanding
Explain in your own words how problems with labour turnover, retention and absenteeism can reduce productivity.

Addressing problems and increasing productivity

Retention problems can be a consequence of PESTLE-related issues. Obviously, if there are skill shortages, employers will have to consider offering higher pay to employees with scarce skills. Absenteeism can reflect weak health care systems and cultural or life-style factors. But there are many other issues that a business can address in practical ways that increase efficiency and productivity.

Incentives

Financial rewards include piecework, commission, bonuses, profit sharing and performance-related pay. All may be used to reward employees who have worked hard. The difficulty with these is that they have to be very carefully thought out so that they actually do provide an incentive. Sometimes employees react to the incentive but not necessarily in a way that increases productivity.

Employee share ownership means that as a shareholder, the employee may want the business to prosper. It may reduce tension between employees and management. But it will only work if the employee shareholder can see potential gains. If the share price is low and dividends are paid infrequently and in small amounts, the effect may be minimal. A small media company tried it, but as soon as the shares had been handed out their price went down to nearly nothing. Employees were unimpressed.

Good communication

Consultation occurs when the management actually engages in discussions with employees about strategies and working practices. German businesses always have Works Councils but there are other approaches. Consultation gives employees a chance to raise issues; managers can help to develop employee understanding of their problems. Consultation is an important element in teamworking. Greater understanding clearly does sometimes help to increase both motivation and productivity.

Empowerment strategies actually involve employees in having a say in decision-making processes; they may also be able to take day-to-day decisions in certain areas.

As with consultation, empowerment can improve morale and foster good teamwork. These can be important elements in a move to increase productivity by introducing new technologies. A combination of different measures can work together in creating a healthy working environment.

Show your understanding
Working with a partner, consider each of the issues below. First identify how this issue is affecting the business (via labour productivity, labour turnover and/or absenteeism). Then decide on suitable strategies to improve efficiency.

1. A receptionist at your local doctors' surgery is very slow when you are booking appointments. He doesn't seem to know how to use the computer system and has to stop regularly to ask for help from a colleague.

2. A secondary school has teacher turnover of 35% per year. Students are complaining that their learning is disrupted by having new teachers all the time. Parents are threatening to send their children instead to a school with a more stable workforce.

3. A window manufacturing firm has experienced recent increases in labour turnover and absence due to injuries associated with manual handling. Most of the injuries are to new recruits who complain that they are having to rush work to meet production deadlines.

Chapter 20
Causes and effects of change

> *"When you're finished changing, you're finished."* – Benjamin Franklin

Dr Gary Hamel is one of the world's most influential business thinkers. He regularly writes for the Harvard Business Review and is on the faculty of the London Business School. When discussing change he says *"You can't build an adaptable organisation without adaptable people, and individuals only change when they have to, or when they want to."*

Think!
Why is change important?
What makes us (a) want change, and (b) avoid change?

External influences

Change happens to all businesses. Sometimes it is internally generated change, but at other times the change is in response to an external opportunity or threat, maybe a PESTLE event. The exact cause, size and effect of the change will of course vary from business to business; therefore, so should the amount of time spent predicting, preparing or reacting. In the mid-1990s, for example, most businesses did not have a website or e-commerce strategy, globalisation was only starting to gather pace and the world was very different. If change is happening all the time how should a business position itself? Do all firms need to be like the Great White Shark, who must hunt continually and will die if it stops swimming? Even Charles Darwin said *"It is not the strongest or the most intelligent who will survive but those who can best manage change."*

If the business environment is constantly changing with different markets changing at different speeds, then businesses need to be adaptable and flexible in order to manage change effectively. Friction occurs when businesses and individuals find change difficult and resistance develops.

Causes of change

Change can be either internal or external. Internal changes tend to be instigated as part of a long term strategy which may reveal strengths and weaknesses. External causes are triggered by opportunities and threats in the business environment. Underlying causes include:

Internal causes	External causes	Action required
Recruitment of new managers	Stronger competition from rival businesses	Market research
Mergers and takeovers		Addressing motivation issues
Buoyant sales leading to growth	The business cycle	Cutting costs: looking for economies of scale, new technologies
R&D leading to new approaches	Rising production costs	
New product developments	Changing customer preferences	Recruiting skilled employees
Weak corporate cultures	New technologies	New product development
Lack of vision in strategic planning	Changes in purchasing power	Attention to product design
Limited motivation		Building a strong culture
	Changes in the law and regulation	

 WATCH OUT!

This chapter requires you to think about most of what you have learnt on this course. You probably know something about nearly everything mentioned in the table above. Now is the time to identify any weak points and do some revision so you can answer the questions about the issues.

Changes in organisational size

Most businesses start off small with an idea or a niche market, but as time passes they will inevitably face decisions about how to grow. Successful growth strategies require change. Consider Google, which went from a two person outfit running from a garage in the mid-1990s to a company with 70 offices in 40 countries employing over 60,000 people. On average, Google has bought two companies a month since 2010.

Growth

Growth allows a business to achieve better control of its cost base and to take advantage of economies of scale. Employee motivation could help or hinder the change. if the business is considering either selling or producing in new countries, communication, recruitment and training will be crucial. The management will need to learn about relevant cultural factors.

> **Find out**
> What aspects of the Google culture would have helped its growth process?
>
> **Discussion points**
> What external factors helped Google to grow?
>
> How important is market research as part of a growth strategy?
>
> Identify three theories you have learnt about that are relevant to a business seeking growth. Think of a business you know about and explain how it might use one of these theories in order to grow.

Poor performance

It is fairly obvious that if a loss making business does not turn itself around, it will fail. But if turning around were that easy, every business would be doing it and there would be no failures. Managers will need to identify the causes of poor performance and consider whether they are symptomatic of underlying problems or simply a one-off anomaly caused by a bad year. Changes take time to implement, and a business which simply lurches from one crisis to another is essentially unsustainable. So devising a strategy requires a thorough analysis of the associated risks and rewards. UK bakery chain Greggs, for example, suffered falling sales until it revamped its product range and broadened its target market. It is now in a strong position to grow further.

Implementing change

Change can bring about startling improvement. Action could involve implementing new technologies, new product development, better training, new recruitment strategies, moving to a taller or flatter management structure, intensive market research and expansion to reap economies of scale. Attention to motivation and leadership issues may be needed; many other possibilities may exist and culture changes may underpin the entire strategy.

> **BHS**
>
> **Restructuring**
>
> On 25th April 2016 British Home Stores collapsed into administration, leading to a potential loss of 11,000 jobs and closure of 163 stores. How did such an iconic brand fall from grace? Was it just another high street casualty destined to fail or was it a case of too little, too late? Opening in 1928 in Brixton, selling clothing and household goods at very reasonable prices, it was an immediate success. By 1931 it was listed on the stock exchange (i.e. become a plc). In 1985 it started expanding into the EU and the Middle East. In 1986 it merged with Habitat and Mothercare to become Storehouse plc. In 2000, Sir Philip Green took it private, buying all the shares; in 2009 he took it into his Arcadia Group alongside Topshop and Burtons, Miss Selfridge and others. The restructuring deals helped to make Green and his wife very wealthy.
>
> Despite repeated attempts at rebranding and relaunching, the company struggled to make profits. It was increasingly becoming a drain on the group finances with losses of £19.3m in 2013 rising to £21m in 2014. So, in 2015, BHS was sold to Retail Acquisitions, a group of financiers, lawyers and accountants, for £1.

Discussion points

How would you account for the poor performance of BHS?

Identify potential strategies that might have helped BHS to stay solvent. Could BHS have been saved by change?

New ownership

Going public

Ownership changes for a number of reasons. There may be a takeover or merger, as in the case of Kraft and Cadbury; such changes in ownership can affect the operational strategy of the business. It could be that a business has been brought in to a conglomerate portfolio for strategic reasons. Tata, the Indian conglomerate, bought Jaguar Land Rover for £1.3bn with the intention of selling the British made cars to the emerging markets of India and China.

Changes in ownership often go hand in hand with changes in size. Many businesses as they grow will think about whether to float their shares on the stock market, allowing much needed access to capital for future growth. However, transferring ownership into the hands of shareholders implies a divorce of ownership and control. The investors (shareholders) may look for short-term gains while the management want to pursue a long-term growth strategy.

Example

Eric Friedman and James Park have taken Fitbit from a Nintendo-inspired hardware start-up company to a profitable gadget maker. They transferred ownership with an Initial Public Offering (IPO) in 2015; this raised $732m. Friedman saw the benefits of having shareholders to please, saying *"You're insanely focussed on hitting the numbers you're guiding everybody to. It gives everyone a clear goal to shoot for."* At the same time the company has maintained its long-term focus: in 2015 it spent $150m on R&D.

Rationalising

Inorganic growth can cut costs by rationalising, creating a single departments for each business function, reducing role duplication in marketing, recruitment, accounting, design and other overhead functions. Other economies of scale may follow. However, efforts must be made to avoid culture clashes and communications need careful handling. Branding changes may be needed.

Sometimes weak performance ends in a management buyout. This happens when managers can see a future for the business despite past losses. They may be highly motivated and the current owner may be willing to sell the business for a low price because of its poor track record. This happened at the Wensleydale Creamery of Wallace and Gromit fame.

Transformational leadership

Being a Chief Executive is hard. Convincing nervous shareholders that your company is actually in a good position requires a cool head, particularly if you have been hired with the sole aim of saving, revitalising or transforming a failing or stagnating business. Transformational leaders tend to focus on the short to medium term and can make the tough decisions required to rejuvenate the business. Harriet Green took over the helm at Thomas Cook at a time of falling sales because of the rise of online travel platforms and the global recession. She said that having a pair of 'fresh eyes' meant she could be objective. By cutting stores and focussing online she seems to have changed the fortunes of the company. Shares bought for 21p in 2012 would be worth 93p now.

Culture

Transformational leaders can change the culture of the business. They can preserve strengths, collaborating with subordinate specialists to identify and solve real problems and boosting morale and motivation at every level.

The market and other external factors

The business environment

The external business environment affects almost all businesses and there will be continual small scale changes that require action. Suppliers change prices, exchange rates fluctuate and minimum wage legislation changes. These and other small changes are unlikely to require strategic thinking but they cannot be ignored. External shocks such as national or global recessions are potentially more damaging. Managers need to understand the effects on the business, and decide how to respond. It may be important to look at the actions competitors are taking and their consequential impact on the business: the knock-on effects. In a recession, mergers can help businesses to survive periods of low sales revenue by rationalising production. Equally, some businesses have survived recession by seeking out new markets to which they can export.

Show your understanding

Transformational change resulted from the adoption of lean production methods in many businesses. When Nissan set up in Sunderland, its success was plain for all to see. Of course, lean production needs to be implemented with careful considerations of the needs of the individual business. Using Nissan (or another business that adopted similar techniques) as an example, explain why this change was so successful.

The effects of change

Change does not just happen to failing businesses. Many businesses hold to the 'why fix it if it isn't broken?' philosophy but they are unlikely to maximise their potential. Far better to seek imaginative solutions – as 3M did, putting in place a programme which allows employees to spend 15 per cent of their time on 'passion projects'. Many of these new ideas are adopted.

However, change may involve risks and businesses should be aware of the effects of change on their competitiveness, productivity and financial performance. Careful change management is called for if the business is to progress. Success can be measured in terms of efficiency gains. But if the actual effects are to be close to the predicted effects, the managers have to identify the real problems and the best solutions before action is taken.

Being adaptable

Businesses in dynamic markets must be very nimble, capable of reacting to change quickly and appropriately. In a fast moving and competitive business environment, a culture in which being flexible and adaptable is the norm confers huge benefits. Change is likely to be accepted as normal.

Competitiveness

Successful companies, as we have seen, grow and change over time. They examine and evaluate every aspect of their business to keep it as efficient as possible. They need to be alert to what competing businesses are doing because they can never stand still for very long. They need foresight and an ability to evaluate risks so that they can innovate without losing sales.

Example

Life in the clothing industry shows how important adaptability is to being competitive. BHS achieved great success over many years by providing fairly 'conservative' products at keen prices and aimed at a distinct demographic. In time, BHS found that whilst sales to females aged 55 and over remained constant, other customers had been lured away by the likes of John Lewis, Zara, H&M, Primark and TK Maxx. There was little in a BHS store that customers could not get elsewhere, either cheaper or more up to date. Zara and H & M change their styles about every six weeks. Primark had the lowest prices, much of the time. By ignoring the customer preferences for fast fashion, BHS lost its competitiveness.

Retail Acquisitions, which bought BHS, appointed a new Chief Financial Officer with a reputation as a 'turnaround expert'. The new management might have been able to help. But the external pressures created by changing customer preferences were just too great.

Competitive-ness

Growth, ownership changes and capable leadership can all increase competitiveness. Poor business performance will almost always be linked to weakening competitiveness. PESTLE factors can defeat even sound businesses, unless they seek competitiveness through a complete change in product or design features.

Productivity

Investment

Improving productivity is usually an implied goal of most businesses; finding a way to increase output without increasing unit costs increases profit. Investment in new technology and training programmes will improve labour productivity. The Nissan plant in Sunderland is seen as the most efficient in Europe and continues to invest, most recently with £100m to build the Nissan Juke. This has guaranteed the future of nearly 7,000 people directly employed as well as a supply chain with over 25,000 employees. Obviously competent management is required to carry such big plans through to success.

The Nissan plant in Sunderland is seen as the most efficient in Europe.

Financial performance

Change is always intended to have a positive effect on financial performance. However this does not always mean making stratospheric profits. Change may be essential simply to survive. Also, profitability may improve quickly. Careful monitoring should be continuous.

> **Example**
> Marks and Spencer Group Plc has a Plan A, the Corporate Social Responsibility Plan, which is a rolling programme covering products, stores and charity work. Since 2007 energy efficiency in all stores has improved by 40% using more efficient technology. Packaging has been reduced by 60%. Despite an increasingly competitive environment, the group was able to increase shareholder dividends in 2015 as pre-tax profit rose to £661.2m.

Stakeholders

Adjusting to change

Change is particularly likely to affect employees and shareholders; both should be kept well-informed of plans for long-term change. Some businesses identify key stakeholders using techniques such as stakeholder mapping (see page 81). This makes it more likely that key stakeholders will have been consulted prior to the launch of the strategy and communicated with throughout.

Judging the effect of external changes on stakeholder groups is more problematic. Similarly a change in working practices because of new legislation may affect employee motivation, productivity or even labour turnover. Raising labour productivity to maintain competitiveness may end in redundancies. Rising input costs may affect prices and therefore customers' purchasing power. Some situations may be favourable for some stakeholders but there is much scope for dispute and disappointment. Communication matters.

> P.S. This book was written shortly before the EU referendum. There was then, and later, so much uncertainty that it was impossible to say what would happen. But now that we know the result of the referendum, it is clear that many businesses are likely to encounter dramatic changes. Read Chapters 20-22 keeping in mind that their content is very relevant to events occurring in the period 2016-20 and possibly long after that. When you come to Chapter 22, think about scenario planning for the immediate future. Make sure you are always well-informed about the current business environment.

Chapter 21
Key factors in change

Marvel Comics

The company is the iconic home of legendary superheroes such as Iron Man, Spiderman and the Hulk. In 1997 the company filed for bankruptcy after a rollercoaster history, and it looked like the end. A merger with Toy Biz led to the formation of Marvel Enterprises which was then bought by Disney in 2009 for $4bn, causing panic amongst die-hard comic book fans. Would Disney's culture ruin Marvel? Focussing on film franchises such as X-Men and Spider-Man seems to have revitalised the business. The 2002 film Spider-Man earned over $800m and in 2012 The Avengers took over $1 billion in the first two weeks after release. By changing the nature of the business to create the Marvel 'Universe', they developed a strategy which opened up multiple revenue streams from toys to publishing to licensing games. At the same time moving from a niche to a mass market required wholesale change and a deeper understanding of consumer behaviour.

Strategic change

Change can be internally or externally initiated; the effect of the change can be positive or negative, depending on many causal factors. Analysing the effects of strategic change involves identifying key factors in the change process and factors that were less influential. Three critical questions can be asked about the extent to which each of the factors addressed in this chapter influenced:

● the decision to change
● the way the change was implemented and
● the reaction to the change.

Organisational culture

 WATCH OUT!

Make sure you are in full command of work done on corporate cultures (pages 74-8) and the causes and effects of change (Chapter 20). Also revise consultation and empowerment (page 103 and Theme 2).

Resistance to change

Culture is essentially the DNA of a business. It determines not only what decisions are made but how they are made. Some cultures are extremely resistant to change, but equally, the existing culture can be a significant enabler of any kind of change. For example making *structural* changes may not help the business if the underlying problems are *cultural*. If a business wants to become more customer focussed then making structural changes without empowering the workforce to act in a new way is likely to be less successful. On the other hand, if a company can use the energy and emotional commitment that is inherent in its culture, change is more likely to be sustainable. Therefore the role of management is to use the culture to build lasting change rather than trying to go against it.

Different cultures

Think!

The consultancy company Strategy& is part of the accountants, Price Waterhouse Coopers. In 2013 it carried out a culture and change management survey, asking over 2,000 participants worldwide what they thought about company culture and barriers to sustainable change. The results said:

● 84% believed culture was critical to success, and 60% thought it more important than strategy

● Only 35% thought their company culture was effectively managed

● The top barriers to change were seen to be competing priorities and having systems and processes that did not support the change.

Interestingly, when asked whether change was sustainable, 70% of participants in Central America agreed, yet only 56% in North America agreed and 40% in Europe.

1. Based on your understanding of different types of culture, which one do you consider to be the most likely to influence change positively? Explain your answer, referring to supporting case studies.

2. In what ways did Disney change the Marvel culture? Apply the three questions above to your answers.

The extent to which the culture is a key factor in building and implementing change also depends on how deeply the culture and values run, and how entrenched the culture is. This is also linked to the size and scale of the operation. For example, how much do the employees at the lower end of a hierarchical, global business embrace the same culture and values shown by top management? Would changing the organisation have the same effect on every member of staff?

Size of organisation

Change, as we have seen, is riddled with the unknown and the unexpected, and managing change is a little like launching a rocket into space. Despite meticulous preparation a multitude of factors can influence the outcome, causing the rocket to veer off course, take longer to reach its destination, or become lost in orbit, perpetually going nowhere. Given this level of risk many leaders of large organisations may consider 'no change' to be the safest option. A recent Harvard Business Review article said that whilst 80% of executives recognised the need for change, only 33% were confident that the change could actually be implemented in the medium term. That said, the Marvel Comics story suggests success is possible.

Many large, older organisations have recognised the increasing pace of change; some have pioneered change and others are now playing catch up. Businesses realise that investment in technology alone is no longer adequate and that the workforce must accept change as the norm rather than the exception. They are slowly transforming the way they operate. Gary Hamel, management guru, says "The most profound business challenge we face today is how to build organisations that change as fast as change itself."

Collaboration

The size of the business has an undoubted impact on any strategic change, and if we apply the law of unintended consequences then changing one part of an organisation may end up improving one area whilst creating adverse effects in another. The larger a business is, the more important it is to co-ordinate the change effectively. Otherwise the business will become disjointed and lack of effective collaboration between departments may create costly problems.

Time and speed of change

Think!

Disrupters are businesses that bring about major changes in competitive markets. In the digital world, 'disrupt or be disrupted' has become a mantra. Digital disruption refers to changes enabled by digital technologies that disrupt the established approaches to value creation, social interaction, doing business and setting strategy. Can any business immunise itself or is having a digital strategy vital in todays business world?

Transformation

Managers who want to embrace the idea of digital disruption need to create agility within their business. If they delay decisions or are too risk adverse, they are unlikely to be able to respond to dynamic market conditions. Harvard Business Review suggests that the success rate of major corporate change programmes is around 30%. Apparently businesses do not understand the difference between change and transformation. Essentially, change is about making a difference to the way things are done. Transformation on the other hand is about reinventing the organisation, based on a vision for the future and a clear expectation that the business will take advantage of upcoming opportunities.

Shorter product life cycles

Of course, change does not happen overnight; all the time a business is seeking to change, the external environment itself continues to change. It is crucial that both the timing and the speed of change are carefully assessed. There is no point in taking advantage of an opportunity if the time taken to implement the change is longer than the time the window of opportunity stays open. As change continues, product life cycles tend to shorten, especially in technology companies. Changes need to happen faster; the business needs to be willing and able to move quickly.

> **Example**
>
> Across the world, a battle is being fought between 'traditional' taxi companies and the new firms on the block, the most high profile of which is the disrupter, Uber. From London to Los Angeles these companies have shaken the market by its roots and are being met with heavy resistance, but in an environment of change their resistance is largely futile. Traditional taxi drivers are complaining about Uber's 'illegal' activities saying their drivers do not have official permits and can't charge by the kilometre as their vehicles don't have metres. Is it a case of traditional companies being in denial, stuck in a system that no longer exists, or do they have a legitimate point? In a *Financial Times* interview one London cab driver said "We were here before Uber and we will be here long after."
>
> Interestingly, however, some policy-makers are supporting the taxi companies' resistance. Uber has been hit by court injunctions in Belgium, France, Germany, the Netherlands and Spain. Taxi driver protests against Uber have clogged the streets in major European cities. However, following protests by taxi drivers in June 2014, Uber saw an 850% increase in new users. The company is currently worth $40 billion and seems here to stay.

Taxi driver protests against Uber have clogged the streets in major European cities.

Managing resistance to change

Klaus Keinfeld, CEO of Alcoa said *"The biggest limiting factor is not technology anymore, it's the humans in the organisation that are not used to questions."* This suggests that any change that does not include consideration of the human resources element will be more difficult to implement. The Strategy& research suggested that employees are resistant to change if they do not feel involved, do not understand the reasons, and have experienced failed changes in the past. Of course employees are not the only stakeholder group. But if businesses do not manage stakeholder expectations during and after change, the changes may fail as efforts are abandoned and resistance grows.

Think!
Kotter and Schleisinger set out the following six approaches to dealing with resistance to change:

Education and Communication – which must happen before and during the change.

Participation and Involvement – by using techniques such as stakeholder mapping (see page 81).

Facilitation and Support – by understanding that resistance will occur and being proactive.

Negotiation and Agreement – offering incentives to support rather than resist change.

Manipulation and Co-option – allowing those who resist to have a voice.

Explicit and Implicit Coercion – forcing people to accept change if speed is the key.

Involvement

Generally speaking, resistance occurs when the change is not shared, interpreted well, or understood. The most effective managers realise that resistance is a natural reaction to change and needs careful management. It can happen because of:

- General dislike of change.
- Fear or uncertainty, especially about possible redundancies.
- Perception of negative consequences.
- Attachment to current culture.
- Lack of agreement that change is needed.
- Lack of clarity about individual contribution to the change.

Uncertainty

This resistance can be magnified if stakeholders experience too much change, or a series of failed changes. Therefore if business leaders plan for resistance, involving key stakeholders and developing a culture of trust and openness, the change has more chance of success.

A report by Deloitte 'Global Human Capital Trends' found that half of the companies questioned were currently restructuring, and this means putting more emphasis on teamwork. Through consultation and empowerment, teamwork fosters employee engagement and increases the scope for improved motivation. This model is replacing the traditional company hierarchy and allows for quicker change. John Chambers, Chairman of Cisco says "we compete against market transitions, not competitors. Product transitions used to take five or seven years, now they take one or two."

Restructuring

However, developing teams in itself needs careful management, otherwise it could actually add to the resistance. Jeff Bezos, leader of Amazon is a good example of an opportunity-driven leader who spearheads change in the organisation. He said "If I see more than two pizza boxes for lunch, the team is too big." By keeping teams focussed on the goal but building in flexibility, so that people have more control over their working lives, they will feel more empowered and therefore likely to accept change.

Teamwork

Show your understanding
1. Using the three questions on page 109, show how the size and culture of Disney's organisation affected Marvel's change process.

2. Explain the significance of these key terms for businesses contemplating change: teamwork, flexibility, consultation, empowerment, employee engagement, motivation.

Chapter 22
Scenario planning

Contingency planning

Think!

"The present moment used to be the unimaginable future."

– Stewart Brand 'The Clock of the Long Now'

Scenario planning, sometimes also known as contingency planning, is the philosophy of asking "what if?" questions about the business environment. It is a strategy that challenges the assumption that tomorrow will be the same as today; it guards against potentially negative outcomes. The theory says that by trying to make sense of an uncertain future the business will make better decisions today. In a complex and fast moving business environment, dealing with uncertainty is one of the key drivers of business success. Shell, for example, has used scenario planning since the 1960's and in doing so has avoided bankruptcy on several occasions.

Scenario planning is about looking beyond what is possible today, into the realm of what is plausible tomorrow. This helps the business to judge how much it needs to change to take advantage of opportunities, or spend to protect itself against threats. Of course when considering the value of scenario planning, quite likely problems are easier to plan for than distant and less likely disasters. Creating accurate expectations about situations that are improbable but possible is rather hard. Even Bill Gates got it wrong when, in 1981, he said "640K (of RAM) ought to be enough for anybody."

Identifying key risks through risk assessment

Quantifying risks

An understanding of the nature of risk is vital for any business. Risks can be quantified – probabilities can be calculated using accumulated data. Uncertainty cannot be treated in this way – it is not quantifiable. Scenario planning makes use of known probabilities while also examining the consequences of uncertain outcomes.

The 2015/2016 floods in the UK

Kate Claughan owns The Book Case in Hebden Bridge, West Yorkshire. On Christmas Day 2015 she heard the flood siren in the valley where she lived. Two days later when she entered her shop there was complete devastation. Bookcases, shelving, desks and computer equipment were all damaged beyond repair. Ms Claughan estimated the flooding cost her business around £50,000 including stock and loss of trade. Even more frustrating was the fact that after the 2012 floods the shop had invested in specialist wall coverings, a new flood door and a flood gate. Ms Claughan says the business is now uninsurable, commenting *"We have been putting money away for when it floods again. It's self-insurance and seems common sense."*

The aftermath of the floods in Hebden Bridge.

Discussion point

Scenario planning led Kate to invest in protective measures which seemed worthwhile. But the insurance company backed off. Explain both actions.

Businesses need to consider the possible risks, assess the likely cost of their happening and estimate the probability of their occurring.

● In assessing the financial risk, the actual cost associated with unexpected events, the business may use Ansoff's Matrix; diversification may protect them from a scenario in which one product faces fast falling sales. Investment appraisal might show the likely risk and reward in improving safety.

Reputational risk

● Assessing reputational risk, the business may need to examine how perceptions might be affected if a product develops faults. Businesses devote huge sums to nurturing their brands and building a strong reputation, so product failures can be very costly. Prevention may be worth considering.

> **Example:** Richard Branson's Virgin Galactic project. The Virgin Group has invested heavily in the project but not to the extent where it's failure would bring down every element of the company. On the other hand if Virgin Galactic were to fail, the reputation of the Virgin brand could be negatively affected.

Risk is a natural feature of business. Whilst avoiding risk may be pointless, assessing and managing risk is not. Businesses should focus on understanding the risk and their capability to respond and manage the risk. Adopting this approach, businesses should be better able to make strategic decisions that maintain their competitiveness.

The key question is how much time, effort and money a business should spend on risk assessment scenario planning. One simple hypothesis may help them to evaluate the benefits:

> Strategic importance of risk = Likelihood of risk occurring + Financial implications of risk occurring

Natural disasters

The UK suffers fewer natural disasters than some other parts of the world. Some USA businesses take out earthquake insurance as part of their normal business costs. However natural disasters do occur; they are notoriously difficult to plan for due to uncertain timing and severity but businesses should not ignore the risk. However an agricultural business, for example, may be affected more immediately and more severely by a period of prolonged drought than a bank. Crop insurance is an option for farmers. Each business must assess its own vulnerability. Some, like Kate in the flood case study, will find that the insurance company has made its own decision.

IT systems failure

Most businesses use IT in some capacity, whether for advertising, communication, record keeping or as a means of distributing the product (as with digital downloads). The risk of IT failure will have different implications depending on the size of the business and the way IT is used.

Measuring cost

It is, of course, very difficult to assess the likelihood of IT failure and the consequential cost. Making a judgement about how much money to spend or save 'just in case' must be based on a thorough understanding of the business and the market. Measuring the cost of losing a day's sales is fairly easy; this can be compared with the cost of replacing key elements in the IT system. Quantifying the potential loss of reputation resulting from an IT failure is more problematic.

One of the biggest problems in assessing the risk of IT failure is that many businesses depend on other organisations for IT services. They cannot control internet connection speeds or interruptions on a certain day. They can attempt to measure the level of likelihood and impact, based on past experience, but cannot expect total accuracy.

The risk of IT failure has different implications depending on the size of the business and the way IT is used.

ICT systems and banking

There can be few things more frustrating than wanting to withdraw money from a bank and not being able to do so, but where does the fault lie? In 2016 the chair of the UK's Treasury Select Committee, Andrew Tyrie, said that the Bank of England should take a leadership role in addressing the systems failures that have caused problems for customers. He said "...every few months we have yet another IT failure at a major bank...These IT blunders and weaknesses are exposing millions of people to uncertainty, disruption and sometimes distress. Businesses suffer too." This came after HSBC customers were locked out of their accounts for two days in January 2016.

A high profile IT failure occurred when Royal Bank of Scotland customers were affected for some weeks in 2012. The company had to pay a £56 million fine to the PRA (Prudential Regulation Authority). RBS continued to suffer problems in 2013 but this time as a result of cyber-attacks.

Towards the end of 2015 complaints about Vodafone soared. The company had installed new customer billing software and blamed the problems on a 'glitch'.

Discussion point

Some analysts point to two causes of IT systems failure. Firstly there is continued under-investment, but secondly they say mergers and acquisitions make IT systems more complex and prone to failure. What options might a scenario planning group consider and why?

Loss of key staff

In all organisations there will be some members of staff who are absolutely integral to the working of the company; their absence will negatively affect the working of the business. In a small organisation, for example, there may be just one person who maintains the ICT network and has very specific knowledge. The consequences of this one person being absent are potentially damaging. Businesses should therefore assess human resource risks such as death, disability or employees quitting. Whilst it would, of course, be nonsense to try and judge the probability of these occurrences, it is possible to assess their impact. The organisation may use this assessment to decide pay and bonus levels. If a firm's legal specialist says they will quit if their workload is increased, the business will need to weigh up the costs of replacement and loss of specialist knowledge against the cost of meeting their requirements.

Planning for risk mitigation

Reducing exposure

Mitigation can be defined as the action of reducing the severity, seriousness or painfulness of something. Risk cannot be eliminated but risk mitigation reduces exposure to it. There is often a positive correlation between the size of the risk and the size of the reward. The best strategies are those that acknowledge and manage risk, rather than fight it.

BP oil spill preparedness and response

BP state that although they include oil spill prevention as one of their priorities, they acknowledge that spills still happen. This allows them to focus on control, containment and clean up. By carrying out simulation exercises, investing in response capability and continually modifying oil spill response plans, they say their ability to respond to events has improved over time. BP measure the number of oil spills per year where the volume is greater than one barrel (159 litres or 42 gallons). They said this figure fell from 74 spills in 2013 to 55 spills in 2015.

Show your understanding

1. Calculate the percentage reduction in oil spills between 2013 and 2015.

2. Are oil spills inevitable? Discuss the strategic decisions BP would have to make when planning for risk mitigation.

Survival

Business continuity

Essentially the goal of any exercise in risk assessment and scenario planning should be to ensure the long term survival of the business. The most elementary research will reveal businesses that have failed because they did not predict likely market changes. Companies like Comet, Compaq, Woolworths and Borders exhibit the pitfalls of underestimating the risks they faced. Conversely, Richard Branson and the Virgin Group had a failure rate of just 14 of the 100 or so businesses that the company started. You could argue that this is evidence of how mitigating the risks is more beneficial than eliminating (or ignoring) them. The BCI (Business Continuity Institute) defines continuity as the 'capability of the organisation to continue delivery of products or services at acceptable predefined levels following a disruptive incident.'

Continuity management

The UK Government has produced a continuity management toolkit for business. This shows firms how to identify the key areas likely to be most affected by unexpected events. It asks them to break down the issues into short, medium and long term and how to measure the Maximum Tolerable Period of Disruption (MTPD) and the Recovery Time Objective (RTO). Having done this for premises, technology, information and stakeholders, the business can have a set of plans prepared for any eventuality.

Disaster recovery

Example

Mirus IT and disaster recovery
Mirus IT has over 10 years' experience in working with small and medium-sized businesses. It provides IT support to firms in London and Milton Keynes. One area they specialise in is business continuity and disaster recovery. Their service includes full backup storage and systems recovery in the event of server failure or data loss. Their pricing method is to charge a monthly fee rather than a large initial investment.

Succession planning

Over the course of your studies you will have looked at recruitment and selection, and should be able to discuss the advantages and disadvantages of internal and external recruitment. Succession planning takes the process a stage further: it does not wait for positions to become vacant before developing and preparing staff for key roles. The basic definition from the CIPD (Chartered Institute of Personnel Development) is:

"Succession planning is the process of identifying and developing potential future leaders or senior managers, as well as individuals, to fill other business-critical positions, either in the short- or the long-term. In addition to training and development activities, succession planning programmes typically include the provision of practical, tailored work experience relevant for future senior or key roles."

Transition

Succession planning is about investing in the future of the business to ensure that the firm is not affected negatively during a transition period, such as when a manager leaves and is replaced. Taking time to develop the skills of potential leaders from within the organisation can ensure that there is no disruption to the culture or values of the business. However it is unwise to assume that all members of staff are equally ambitious. The fact that someone is a valued member of the company does not mean they automatically want to be CEO. Good succession planning therefore acknowledges this and in addition to developing the leaders of tomorrow, also nurtures the talent that exists today.

Think!
The co-founder and CEO of Apple, Steve Jobs, planned his succession for years, and built up a large knowledge base of instructional material to help the company continue after his tenure. Tim Cook, his successor, was also groomed to take over for many years. What might have happened to Apple without this careful preparation?